ATHEISM AS A POSITIVE SOCIAL FORCE

ATHEISM AS A POSITIVE SOCIAL FORCE

SOCIAL FORCE

Raymond W. Converse

Algora Publishing
New York

Library of Congress Cataloging-in-Publication Data:

Converse, Raymond W.
  Atheism as a positive social force / Raymond W. Converse.
  p. cm.
  Includes bibliographical references.
  ISBN 0-87586-211-X (pbk. : alk. paper)
  ISBN 0-87586-212-8 (alk. paper)
  1. Atheism—History. 2. Religions—History. I. Title.

BL2747.3.C64 2003
211'.8—dc21
                            2003001950

TABLE OF CONTENTS

INTRODUCTION

The common definition of an atheist is pretty perfunctory: "one who denies or disbelieves in the existence of God." But atheism has its own value as a way of life; it is not only significant as a philosophical position held in opposition to religion. Without a doubt the most important concern of atheism is: What would atheism propose to replace the existence of God? The simple, usual definition is actually of very little use.

The majority of this work will be an attempt to set forth the major lines of philosophical argument that support the position of atheism in a world which still believes, and lives as if, God exists and directs the workings of the world. In the course of this presentation it will also be necessary to set forth the major philosophical arguments of those who rely upon religion as the support of their belief in the existence of God. As the two counter positions are presented, it is hoped that the contrast between them will open the doors to debate.

A few introductory remarks concerning the position of atheism will set the stage for this dialectic. Atheism as it exists today consists of three major schools. The first school consists of people (and they seem to be in the majority) who accept the position that God does not exist. They do not, however, give much more thought to this acceptance. They continue to live their lives as if God does

1

exist. This position does not require much thought or conviction; and if pressed, those who stand on this acceptance would be unable to justify their belief.

The second school consists of those who accept the fact that God does not exist and who are also capable of setting forth a fully thought-out statement of their position. The second school, however, does not take a public stance on their beliefs or convictions. They have replaced God, as the effective author of the world, with human reason. Human reason is equated with the results that have been set forth in the fields of science and technology. This position is based upon a philosophical system of thought known as materialism. This position came into existence, as concerns Western European civilization, within a time period of a few hundred years. The important point here is that the holders of this position do not tend to take a public stance with their position. Science over the last couple of centuries has proposed a series of theories based upon material facts that would argue against the necessity for the existence of God. The theory of evolution, the Big Bang theory, the Theory of Relativity, and the findings of scientific psychology would all fall in this category. Taken together, these theories can be seen as offering an alternative explanation for the beginning of the universe, the continued operation of the universe, and an explanation for each individual member of the universe. Should those theories be proven to a point of certainty, then the need for God and the supernatural generally would be completely negated.

The problem is that most of the theories offered by science have not been proven to that point of certainty. It must also be remembered that belief in the existence of God and the supernatural is only one part of the role that is played by what we know as organized religion. In fact, belief in the explanations of science are seen by those who wish to impugn them as requiring just as great a leap of faith as a belief in God. We will look at this claim later.

In the third category are those (relatively few!) people who not only claim to be atheists and are able to offer fully developed explanations for their atheism, but who also structure their lives to fit their atheism. They are able to, and do, attempt to teach the philosophical position of atheism to those who care to listen. This is, of course, the most difficult position to maintain of the three. It requires not only a working knowledge of religion, but also of science and technology. It is my position that individuals can truly be considered atheist only if they have gotten to this stage; and I hope that this work will bring those who are interested to the point at which such a decision can be made in earnest.

The methodology of atheism is important in our consideration of the position, and the reader is invited as we go through the following chapters to return periodically and review the methodology. The method chosen will consist of three parts. First, it must be understood that the denial found in atheism is not just the denial of God and religion, but is in addition the denial of the supernatural in any form. Second, it will be assumed that anyone who wishes to consider himself or herself an atheist will be ready to do the research necessary to fully support his or her position. Third, an atheist, based on the knowledge gained in that phase, will structure his or her life in a manner consistent with that knowledge. An index is provided at the end of the book from which readers will be able to follow the research available to whatever degree of certainty they require. This will allow readers to answer questions that might arise from those who challenge a belief in atheism.

The road to atheism begins with the premise that the supernatural does not exist in any form. Accepting the fact that the supernatural does not exist, what is left for an atheist to rely upon? The answer is human reason. The first step that one must take, in order for human reason to stand as the foundation of atheism, is to define human reason or the rational.

For our purposes, the first requirement of reason begins with the sensations that are received by our sense organs and are then transmitted to our brains. Modern science presents us with a theory that states that the physical sensations, light waves, sound waves, tastes, odors and touch, produce effects upon our sense organs that are then converted into electrical and chemical impulses. These impulses are then conducted to our brains where they are converted into images, either verbal or visual. While this theory has not yet been proven to absolute certainty, it is the most widely accepted theory of the physical process by which reason begins. The actual composition of the impulses that convey the sensations to the brain and their formation into images has still to be fully traced. However, the theory of electrical and chemical conversion from physical data to mental activity is the most widely accepted, and it represents the greatest degree of certainty that can be obtained in our current stage of knowledge. The sense organs are constantly bombarded with sensations of every type. The sense organs, however, are each limited to a small range of physical data that they can "read." Initially, therefore, the physical data that can be apprehended is strictly narrowed or filtered to leave only the data that falls within the receptivity capability of the sense organ affected. It is understood that there are small variations between individuals as to how wide this range may be, but essentially we all can "read" the same physical data with our sense organs. For the purpose of this definition, we will also accept as a given that the information received by the sense organs is identical with that which left the object under consideration. This is not to say that the objects which we "observe" through our senses are identical with the actual object; but only that what we received as physical data is exactly what is represented by the object. Thus, we accept that our only knowledge of the world outside of our minds and bodies is that which is represented to us by our sense organs and, in addition to what our sense organs can perceive directly, we must also take into consideration the technologies that have been created by modern science. These technologies allow us to extend the range of sensations that we are able to obtain from the outside world. For example, the microscope allows us to view objects with our sense of sight that would be beyond the natural capacity of our eyes to see. This set of technologies will be considered to be a sort of sixth sense. It must be remembered, however, that these technologies still rely upon our sense organs to get the data to our brains.

The second requirement in defining human reason, or the rational, will involve the process that occurs once the data has reached the brain. Modern science again presents us with a theory as to what happens at that point. The physical data, whether of an electrical or chemical nature, is processed by the brain into either thoughts (ideas), which consist of verbal or visual images, or physical responses. It is not fully understood how this is accomplished. It is also not known exactly how the brain decides which of the physical data received it will acknowledge. As psychology would teach us, some of the data is repressed and thereby removed from our conscious attention, while other data is converted to either images or physical reaction. The index lists sources of scientific research that set forth in detail the theories that we can only touch upon briefly in these pages. For the purposes of this discussion, it is enough to understand that the data received is converted to images by a natural process. All of our mental activity, therefore, is a direct result of the data received and its conversion into images. Once again, there appear to be rather wide variations between individuals concerning the process of converting physical data to thought. The process itself, however, appears to be basically the same in all humans.

There appear to be two different types of mental activity. The one is conscious, that is to say, the individual is aware of the activity produced by the brain. The other is not conscious, that is, the individual is not aware of the activity carried on by the brain. For example, the brain is constantly receiving sensations from the autonomic nervous system and is constantly responding to those sensations. This is what keeps our heart beating, our lungs breathing, etc., without our normally being aware of it. On the other hand, the sensations of hunger that are received from the stomach are brought to consciousness and then the individual hunts for food. This is a very simplistic view of what happens to sensations in the brain, but it will at least be suitable for our definition. Our second requirement, therefore, is to understand that all we know of the world, and ourselves, is the result of the conversion of physical data into visual or verbal images.

Our third requirement involves the development of each individual's understanding of what is brought to consciousness by the brain. Although the thoughts created by the brain appear to be totally random, and totally dependent upon the data received, the brain seems to be capable of making judgments about the thoughts. The brain, through another process that is not totally understood, is capable of putting ideas together through association and producing a judgment about the importance of the information. If it is important enough it will be brought to the individuals attention through a verbal or visual image. The individual is then capable of making further decisions concerning these thoughts with yet further thought. This process does not seem to be totally foolproof, as we are all aware of times in which our responses, or the thoughts produced, were nothing short of inappropriate. Our third requirement, therefore, is that each individual is capable of making judgments concerning the value and importance of the data brought to his or her consciousness by means of a conscious manipulation of the data.

Therefore as a working definition of rational (human reason) we understand the process by which raw data is collected by the individual sense organs, the process by which this data is converted into mental activity, and the conscious reaction of the individual to this mental activity. As the individual develops more control over these processes, they are able to reorganize them into ever more complex systems of thought. The child is capable of recognizing mental activity and responding, but is not capable of reorganizing that information into complex systems. It is through the process of reorganization that the individual becomes aware of the regularity of some sensations and the uniqueness of others. This is the process that makes it possible for a young person to learn to speak, to recognize significant others, to determine what is food and what is not and many other things. At a later level the capability to reorganize information is used to educate the individual. This education can come from any source that is available often enough to create regularity in the data received. This is usually parents, siblings, friends, schools, etc. In this connection the education can be either of high or low quality and quantity. For primitive man it was absolutely essential for survival, as it still is for most of the animal world.

Individually, we come to recognize ourselves as distinct from all other objects early in life. As the reorganization process becomes a regular part of mental activity, individuals become capable of making choices as to how they will react to these objects and the thoughts or the ideas associated with them. The more capable a person becomes in reorganizing data, the more complex become the choices. There seems to be a direct correlation between the amount of knowledge and the complexity of the reorganization process. There is, at the highest level, a limit on the amount of knowledge that can be obtained both as individuals and as a species. For this reason there also may be certain types of data that cannot be completely reorganized, i.e., there may be questions that cannot be answered to any degree of certainty. The individual, however, is not limited to the knowledge that can be obtained individually. As with the senses, the community of knowledge held by the whole of mankind can be used as an extension of the individual's knowledge. Modern society abounds with sources for this knowledge, that is, computers, books, television and many others. Even with all of these sources, the amount of knowledge available to the individual tends to be severely limited.

In contrast to the position set forth above is the alternative position taken by those who believe in God (religion) and the supernatural generally. This position starts from the basic foundation that human reason, or the rational, if it exists at all, exists solely as the means by which man can understand the knowledge given by the supernatural. This knowledge may be in several different forms, i.e., it may be given by a supernatural being directly to man. Hence the belief that the various "bibles," e.g., the Christian Bible, the Talmud, the Qur'an, the Avesta, etc., are the actual "words" of the supernatural and not just the words of man. This notion forms the basis of the argument that one must heed these words, to the letter. The tenets that are contained in those books, and others like them, are not the product of human reason based upon the experience of man reorganized by the human brain into ever larger more complex structures but, rather, are merely delivered to man as eternally true statements of divine fact.

The supernatural being which provides mankind with such eternal truth can be seen to take on many forms. It can be of a type normally found in modern religions, i.e., an omnipotent, omnipresent spirit designated as God, Mithra, Allah, etc. and is usually seen as a "good" spirit. Others can also be known as "evil" spirits, such as the devil, Ahriman, and others. These spirits are normally portrayed as totally bodiless and truly spiritual in nature. The supernatural can also be seen, and has been portrayed in history, as human in form and disposition but equipped with more than human power and ability and immortal life. The delivery of the revelations of the supernatural can also be found in different forms, i.e., they can be delivered by men who have been instructed by the divine, such as the prophets of the Christian Bible, or they may be delivered directly by a disembodied spirit as was the case when contact was made with Moses through clouds and burning bushes. They may also be found in the contact of human beings through a disciplined control of the body, as is found in Hindu asceticism.

All of these forms that have been used by mankind to describe the supernatural have one common feature: the source of this knowledge is beyond the ability of mankind to understand solely by the use of his natural reasoning powers. In other words, if the knowledge that is given by the supernatural had not been given, then mankind would not have this knowledge. The knowledge itself, however, has been given to mankind by this incomprehensible being with the specific intent that it will not only be understood by human reason but that it will be acted upon specifically by human beings. It has been most widely accepted, historically speaking, that the method through which this knowledge came to be understood was through the services of what we now call organized religion. This system consists of many different schools, i.e., Christianity, Judaism, Islam, Hinduism, Toa, and many others. In each of these schools the knowledge given by the supernatural is reorganized by selected individuals (those normally appointed by the supernatural or those claiming special powers of understanding) into a form that is capable of being understood by all mankind. The reorganized or interpreted knowledge is then codified in some manner and stands as the basis of religious belief.

We will see later in what forms this interpreted knowledge has been organized and the differences that are apparent in the various interpretations. In general, however, the system of beliefs that surrounds the interpretation of the original knowledge given by the supernatural represents the differences in the existing organized religions.

In looking at the three religions that have had the most effect on the development of Western European civilization, the scenario holds that the divine knowledge was transmitted to individuals who were chosen directly by the supernatural and who have come to be known as prophets. The main function of the prophets was to deliver the knowledge imparted by the supernatural in a form that could be understood by the reason of ordinary men. This knowledge was then codified into a system by various means, all of which resulted in them being put into written form, hence the Bible, the Talmud and the Qur'an. The knowledge contained in those books has, ever since they were written, been subjected to a great deal of commentary by learned men and some of this commentary has become part of the expansion of the books themselves or has been generally confused with the knowledge contained in the original books. This ongoing commentary, which in essence is additional interpretation of the original knowledge given by the prophets, represents in large part the theology, ritual, and content of the actual organized religions and their "churches."

The last step is the presentation of these organized constructs to the individual adherents of the Church. It is at this point that the knowledge given by the supernatural becomes solidified into an unchanging system of eternal truth. Here the position is taken that the individual believer must accept without question the tenets set forth in the theology of the Church. These tenets usually include an unquestioning belief in the supernatural being that delivered the knowledge, an unquestioning belief in the unerring accuracy of the interpreters of this knowledge, i.e., the prophets, mystics, priests, magic or whatever system is used to originally interpret this knowledge, and the unquestioning belief that the Church has incorporated, by means of faithful interpretation, this knowledge and that it is the sole repository and authority for this knowledge.

The alternative approach to atheism bases all relevant knowledge on the condition of the existence of a supernatural being or a force of some type who (for whatever reason) imparts this knowledge to mankind. The understanding and judgments that are made on the knowledge so received are seen to be the sole responsibility of those either directly chosen by the supernatural or those who can show that they have some special power to understand and make judgments concerning this knowledge. The individual is expected to suspend his own judgment and accept without question that the individuals chosen have interpreted this knowledge accurately and that they should be granted the status of an unchanging authority. That is to say, the individual is not responsible for what he or she believes, or for the actions required by these beliefs, as they represent the will of a supernatural being and are to be accorded the status of universal, eternal truth.In summary, we can distinguish the basic differences between the two alternative approaches. In the atheistic approach, all knowledge is based upon the natural processes by which each individual obtains the data of the senses, the method by which the data is converted to energy and transported to the brain, and the method by which that converted data is reorganized into visual and verbal images. Knowledge is the result of these processes and the further natural process by which the brain is capable of reorganizing these images into ever more complex systems or patterns. This type of knowledge is only limited by the individual's exposure to the raw data available for processing, and by the individual ability to organize this data into complex systems upon which a judgment can be delivered. The natural processes in question can also be seen to be extended in some degree by the modern technologies that expand the ability of the senses to collect raw data. These technologies, such as the ability to write, have also allowed the ability of each individual to be expanded to a community of knowledge potentially embracing the judgment of all men. Under the atheistic position, the individual is expected to take responsibility for the knowledge he or she has and the judgments that he or she makes in regard to that knowledge.

Part One of the following book will concentrate on how today's major religions were founded. It is, of course, impossible in just a few pages to do justice to such a huge swath of human history; yet a bold attempt will be made, for we need some grounding in the basic facts of the religious view if we are to appreciate and evaluate the alternative position, atheism. (Hopefully, the sketch presented will interest readers to seek further information.) A detailed consideration will also be given of the actual content of the various systems that were developed to foster a better understanding of the position of religion — or the supernatural in general. When possible, the position of atheism will be contrasted to the position of religion. In most cases, this can be seen as the author's attempt to set forth the position of atheism if it had actually existed at the time.

Part Two will set forth the position of atheism as a potential force in modern society and how it relates to the issues that seem to be the most salient in the United States. The two sections are intended to stand alone, i.e., they are not intended to be dependent upon each other, but the author wishes to stress his belief that one cannot truly comprehend the atheistic position presented in Part two without knowing at least the basic beliefs of the alternative position.

The most that any individual can hope for is a level of knowledge that will allow him or her enough certainty to support the necessary choices in life. For people to be considered rational, they must be able to explain the positions that they take based upon the knowledge that they actually have available, either personally or through the collected knowledge of mankind. In relation to what follows, an attempt will be made to present the knowledge necessary to become an informed atheist, or at least, a guideline as to what type of knowledge is important to such a decision. The actual decisions and the actions taken by the individual are totally up to the individual.

PART ONE

Chapter 1. The Origin of Religion

In the Introduction, human reason was established as the foundation of the philosophical position known as atheism. The foundation of religion depends not upon human reason but upon revealed knowledge. Revealed knowledge is the belief that God has directly transferred all the knowledge that man has. Most religions base their philosophical position on the direct revelation of God's thoughts to man.

Throughout the vast majority of recorded history, as well as history as we have been able to reconstruct it from pre-historic times, the most important aspect of the individual's life has been religion. It is unlikely that anyone can understate the importance of religion in the development of mankind. The concept of atheism does not include such a vast place in history and it has had a much smaller impact upon the individual. This being true, it seems appropriate to lay down the facts, as known to modern science, concerning the development of religion.

Little can be stated concerning the manner in which the pre-historic peoples conducted their lives and what they believed in connection with that life. What little is known is based on conjecture derived from the remains that have been found by archeologists. One must start with what little is known of the so-called Neanderthal man. The Neanderthal is believed to have been either the direct ancestor to our species or, at least, to have lived during the time of the early development of our species. The archeological record of Neanderthal is very limited indeed. It is speculated that they existed as hunter-gathers and lived in troops of up to 50 persons. A large portion of their diet appears to have been obtained by the hunting of the large game animals that existed at the same time, i.e., mammoths, wooly rhinoceros and others. They were capable of manufacturing large stone points that they used in the hunt. Because they existed in the severe climate of Europe during the last ice age, it is also assumed that they had control of fire and were able to make clothing. They appear to have inhabited caves for at least a portion of the year. If the conjecture that they lived in groups of varying size is assumed to be true, it can also be assumed that they had obtained to a relatively high level of social organization. This would, of course, indicate that they were capable of speech. The use of speech and group organization clearly indicates that they had traveled far on the road of being able to reorganize their thoughts into complex systems. In short, it would appear that, even as early as 50,000 years ago, the Neanderthal was rational by our definition.

It is impossible from the archeological record to determine anything with certitude concerning any beliefs they may have held. What the archeological record does give us is a series of what appear to be intentional burials. The bodies seem to have been deliberately orientated and placed with forethought. They also appear to have been painted with the substance known as red ocher. From these facts, it has been further speculated that the Neanderthal had at least a primitive concept of an after-life. This may have been nothing more than an attempt to prevent the spirits of the dead from coming back to bother the living. It may also have been much more, but it will never be known exactly why they buried their dead. The burials have been generally accepted by science as proof that the Neanderthals had a rudiment of belief in the supernatural, in some form, even if it was a simple type of superstition rather than what we would call religion. Whatever the actual purpose of the intentional burial, it is, at the very least, a sign that they were concerned with the dead. While the archeological record supports the speculations set forth above, it does not support any further speculation.

Between 50,000 and 30,000 years ago, another species of human came into existence. This species was Homo sapiens. Whether this species appeared as an independent development of evolution or evolved from Neanderthal is still under debate. It is not important for our purposes. This species is considered by modern science to be identical to modern man in all important aspects of a physical and mental nature. The earliest known sites that were occupied by modern man have been found in the Near East and in Western Europe. It is clear from these finds that modern man co-existed with Neanderthal for some period of time, early in their history. It is unknown what type of relationship existed between the two species. Some think that the disappearance of Neanderthal was the result of interbreeding with the genetically superior modern man, while others hypothesize that the disappearance of Neanderthal was occasioned by modern man hunting him into oblivion. If the two were actually separate species, they would have been incapable of interbreeding and the second conjecture would remain in force. If they were of the same species and only differed due to genetic mutations, it is unlikely that they were hunted as food. It is possible, however, that the genetic differences led to hatred between the species and the superior capability of modern man led to the destruction of Neanderthal. Either of these last two theories seems tinged with the bias of racial prejudice. Whatever the cause, it was not long before Neanderthal disappeared from the archeological record. Neanderthals at this time had already spread from their original home in Africa to most of what are now Europe, the

Near East, India, Central and South Eastern Asia. It appears that modern man replaced Neanderthal in all of these areas very rapidly.

As stated earlier, there is no direct proof available to indicate the birthplace of modern man as a species. It is also impossible to determine how long the species has been in existence, or even what may have been the routes by which modern man expanded from his original home. What is certain is that modern man became the dominant species, indeed the only species of human, around 28,000 years ago.

The earliest archeological record from this period includes burial sites in the Near East and the cave dwellings of southeastern France. Although the finds in the Near East are not very extensive, they do indicate that modern man had altered his general lifestyle. A completely new type of tool manufacture is evident, along with the now confirmed use of fire. The scientific community has theorized, based on that information, that modern man, at least in the Near East, had converted from a dependence on hunting to food gathering. This theory includes the speculation that mankind may already have entered into the process of domesticating some types of wild grains and animals. It is thought that such activities were limited to the sowing and collecting of wild grains and the use of small animals as additional food sources. These speculations are not a direct part of the archeological record, so it is impossible to set forth the beliefs that may have been a part of this transition. The fact that true early farming and herding techniques appear in this area as early as 16,000 years ago lends a great deal of support to the above theory of modern man's development.

The record in Europe was of a different type. Here, modern man left a type of written record of his activities. This record consists of the paintings on the walls of the caves located in France. The paintings seem to have been made in portions of the caves that were the most difficult to access. This, of course, would mean that a reliable source of artificial light had been created. The paintings show very realistic representations of animals known to have existed at that time in Europe. They also contain representations of the weapons used, and human figures in the action of hunting, as well as outlines of hands with missing fingers. While we cannot know the purpose of the paintings for early modern man, they have certainly inspired several theories. The most widely accepted theory holds that they represent some type of ritual involved with the hunt, a ritual believed to have been a form of primitive magic. The cave paintings, coupled with the finds of burial sites containing weapons and items of every day use, have brought scientists to the conclusion that early modern man was already highly advanced in his beliefs about the supernatural. It is evident that modern man in Europe was still largely engaged in a hunting existence and probably had not made the conversion to dependence on gathering. The paintings clearly show that modern man was rapidly increasing his ability to reorganize the data of the outside world into higher and more complex systems of thought. There is no question that he had mastered the manufacture of tools specifically designed for hunting certain types of game, i.e., small points for hunting birds, fishhooks, etc. There is also no question that he had mastered fire as a source of artificial light, heat, and presumably to cook his food. He also produced clothing suitable to his climate and, most important, he had learned to represent the outside world through the use of his imagination. It is likely that he also used these representations in his attempt to control some aspects of his environment. The paintings also seem to point to the fact that modern man had started upon the use of a division of labor based on talent. The quality of the paintings is such that only a few of those who made up the society could have had the talent to draw them. The same remains true in today's world.

When the accomplishments of modern man both in Europe and the Near East are combined the conclusion cannot be escaped that rationality similar to that of today already existed. The suspected advances in social structure found in gathering societies, the domestication of animals, the representation of reality in painting and many others are all evidence of modern man as rational. Taken as a whole the picture taken from the archeological record shows that great advances in rational organization had occurred over a very short period of time. It also must be remembered, however, that there is very little direct proof supporting the speculations offered by science. They do, however, offer the best explanation that can be obtained under our current state of knowledge.

When the accomplishments of modern man reach the point at which they become a part of a true written record, many questions are answered. The systems that appear in the earliest writings of mankind are complex to a very high degree. It is reasonable to assume that this level could not have been reached without a relatively long period of prior development. It is in this requirement that science finds its strongest support for the theories it presents concerning early man.

Only two conclusions will be accepted here as having been proven to a high degree of certainty. The first is the unquestioned advance in man's ability to reason. The second is that mankind was beginning to develop more complex lifestyles requiring a reorganization of his social skills. It will also be conjectured, but not with certitude, that the cave paintings and burials represent a concern with the supernatural. This would include a concept of an after-life, magic and superstition. In short, mankind had begun to build what would later be known as religion.

The lifestyles associated with the peoples who occupied Europe and the Near East during the period between 12,000 and 6,000 years ago were quite varied. In the Near East the lifestyle became increasing involved with the domestication of plants and animals. This development seems to have taken place in that region for several different reasons. First, the area contained the widest number of plants and animals that would be relatively easy to domesticate, including a wild form of primitive wheat, as well as primitive forms of the modern chicken, goat, sheep and dog. Second was the continued evolution of this area from one of extensive grasslands to one of ever decreasing rainfall.

The result of these two trends seems to have been a rapid increase in the population, as domesticated food sources became more reliable. It is also likely that the increased amount of labor required to grow and maintain domesticated food sources spurred a growth in the social structures needed to provide this labor. It is at this time that evidence of proto-villages and larger tribal organizations begin to appear in the archeological record.

This lifestyle, in its most primitive form, seems to have spread from the Near East into Central Asia, India and Southeast Asia very early in this period. It is supposed that the growth of population in the Near East was relieved by migrations of people to the east. They took with them their knowledge of domesticating wild plants and animals. It is likely that they took the dog and chicken with them. There also seems to have been an early attempt to migrate into North Africa. The migration into Africa seems to have stalled out after reaching Egypt. This may have been the result of environmental factors. The Sahara Desert had already begun to form, or may have already reached close to its current extent. The existing jungle may also have extended northward into the Sudan. Mankind may not yet have reached a level of organization that would allow him to make use of these environments. The migration to the East, however, seems to have continued through India into Southeast Asia and China. The evidence available would indicate that rice and small animals were domesticated in this part of the world as early as 11,000 years ago. The migration even seems to have continued by way of boat into the Pacific islands, including Australia, at about the same time. Rice seems to have been first domesticated from its wild ancestor in India and then was carried to Southeast Asia and China. In the whole region, the domestication of plants and animals seems to have been closely followed by larger and larger social structures. The exception to this theory would be found in the Pacific islands and Australia. Here, environmental conditions may have dictated against this type of development.

The most complete archeological record for these processes is found in the Near East.

By 11,000 years ago, the archeological record begins to show evidence of permanent villages throughout the Near East. The size of the sites that have been found would indicate that they contained as many as several hundred people. The record would also indicate that the villages largely relied upon domesticated plants as their major food source. The size of these sites would indicate that a highly organized social structure existed. This would have included at least a working concern for the division of labor. Later developments would indicate that it also included some type of class structure, a defined leadership of the community and a division of the duties of women and men. The sites seemed generally to have been without walls. This would indicate little contact between the villages or others that may have occupied the area surrounding the villages. Artifacts found at these sites show evidence of a high level of prosperity. There are many different types of utensils found that would have been used in everyday life. There were also items that could have had no use other than decoration. In short, the villages or sites of this time period indicate that the villages were permanent and relatively large, supported a division of labor, and were probably managed by a primitive form of government. These sites show a clear line of development into the sites that contain our earliest written records. Written records first began to appear about 4,500 years later. Over that short period of time, the Near East had gone from villages, herding societies and small cities to large cities, empires and all the trappings that we today call civilization. Whatever the beliefs of the peoples who lived during the initial 4,500 years or so, they were quickly developed into those that are displayed in the earliest writings. It is fair to assume that all that existed at the time writing appeared also existed in some less-developed form during this whole period. This would mean that religion had already obtained its present form with only a few minor exceptions.

The second lifestyle that developed during this period seems to have its origins either in Europe or the Russian steppes at the end of the last extension of the glaciers. As the intermediate period gained strength, the glaciers began to recede northward. In their wake they seem to have left an environment that was wetter and warmer than what we find there today. This environment covered most of the southern half of Europe, the Russian steppes and southern Siberia, most of Central Asia and northern China; it supported large herds of grazing animals on new grasslands. The herds consisted of mammoth, rhinoceros, giant bison, giant sloth and others. The second lifestyle developed in order to hunt these animals efficiently. This lifestyle required a high level of mobility: the grazing animals moved over great amounts of territory and the people who hunted them moved with them. There is no evidence of semi-permanent or permanent villages during the early portion of this period. This lifestyle does not seem to have changed much between 16,000 and 10,000 years ago. It consisted of small groups of people who maintained temporary camps along the migration routes of the large game animals.

The population growth that seems to have occurred during the peak period for the large game animals seems to have promoted the development of larger social units at the end of this period. These were carried over into the new environment in the form of tribes. This type of organization included the use of semi-permanent or in some cases permanent villages. It also included a more highly developed social structure, with its growing need for social division and control. The institution of the social process which led to tribal organization and social structures seems to have already have taken place prior to the migrations to the American continents. Although little is directly known about the organization of these peoples, this lifestyle seems to have been fairly stable. It also seems to have existed at a much lower level of material prosperity and social organization than the contemporary societies in the Near East. The areas currently under consideration vary greatly, depending on the time frame involved and the specific area concerned. As the environment became increasing more like that which exists today, the large game animals began to disappear. The generally accepted theory is that a combination of over-hunting by man and an increasingly difficult environment led to their extinction. During this period, the vast forests of Europe and the somewhat less bountiful grasslands of Russia and Central Asia developed. This new environment supported large numbers of animals. In Europe, the forests supported herds of deer and other forest animals. In Russia and Central Asia, smaller herd animals such as the horse, and several forms of cattle, developed. In Europe, man still depended to a large degree upon hunting but supplemented his food sources with the gathering of nuts and other foods. In Central Asia, the periodic contact with peoples on the fringe of their territories who had already domesticated small herd animals led to a society totally dependent upon herd animals.

A picture of the general lifestyle will be drawn from the limited amount of archeological material available. It is not possible to use the later written record concerning the minimal contacts between those who could write and those who did not. It is possible, however, to draw some support from the American tribes as they existed when Europeans made first contact. The same would be true of the historical peoples who lived a similar lifestyle in Africa, the Pacific islands and in Australia. It is believed that the lifestyle generally consisted of a slow conversion from a total dependence on hunting to one that included a larger dependence on gathering, some domestication of plants (agriculture) and in some areas on herd animals. Each tribe seems to have had a relatively defined territory that they considered their own and which they were willing to defend. The tribe seems to have contained a small number of people when compared to the villages and cities developing in the Near East. The tribes that existed in adjacent areas, however, do appear to periodically have joined together in larger units known as hordes. The tribal system seems to have been very closed, i.e., each tribe developed its own system of leadership, its own religious beliefs, division of labor and way of life.

Although the belief in the supernatural cannot be directly shown from the archeological record, science has been able to offer a theory as to its general outlines. This theory has been constructed from the early written records and the beliefs of primitive peoples encountered by Europeans. The actual beliefs seem to have varied widely among the various tribes. There are, however, some points in which they all seemed to agree. This has led to a theory known as primitive religion. The major lines of agreement include a tendency to invest all objects, both animate and inanimate, with a spirit of its own; a belief that the spiritual world was capable of affecting the human world, its actions seen as either good or bad depending on whether they aided or hindered mankind in his survival; and the construction of a pantheon of gods and goddesses. Each god and goddess was associated with some aspect of the natural phenomena that affected the tribe. Each tribe, depending on the lifestyle it adopted, assigned the gods and goddesses to the phenomena that were the most important for their survival: the sun, moon, rain, wind, etc. Lastly, the gods and goddesses were seen to be in close personal contact with the individuals that made up the tribe. As with the agricultural societies, life seems to have become constantly more complex for the tribal societies.

Here also there was a division of labor between the men and the women, the men concentrating of hunting and herding, while the women did most of the gathering and family chores. The division was less extensive than in the agricultural societies, especially in the area of social organization. The religious leaders quickly developed rituals that were intended to influence the manner in which the gods and goddesses were to act. The use of magic (in the sense of household gods) effected the same result with the lesser spirits. This has been described as the stage at which taboos and totems were established; these, and the ritual attached to them, controlled every aspect of the life of the individual within the tribe and represented the social cement that bound the members to each other.

When we look at the development of the two separate lifestyles prior to the appearance of written records, several major trends become apparent. Rapid growth in social structures was needed to cope with the increasing labor, in terms of both time and the numbers of people, that was required to produce food. The larger social units also occasioned a greater need for methods that would hold these units together. This problem was met by the formation of specific forms of leadership that eventually evolved into the forms of government that are familiar to us today. They were also met by the formation of organized primitive religion in both regions. In both cases, the people who actually ran the government or religious structures became a class unto themselves. In short, over a period of some 50,000 years, mankind had developed from small groups of individuals ruled by the strongest male, surviving almost exclusively under the influence of instinct, to a lifestyle that consisted of large groupings dominated by the use of human reason. This process had obtained to a very high degree, as we shall see, by the time written recordkeeping came into use. In these pages we can only trace the barest of outlines concerning the development of mankind over that period of 50,000 years, and it is hoped that readers will be intrigued enough to seek out some of the many books that can provide the intellectual background to make sense of what the physical, archeological record shows actually happened in the actions of mankind, as would be required in a full treatment of religion as a rational occurrence.

What can be portrayed of this vast period of development is mankind's gradual progress in the area of life skills. From the beginning, mankind was organized into larger social units, whether forced, or to some degree by voluntary action, and therefore he had to create the institutions that would support increasingly larger organizations. The archeological record supports, at the very least, the idea that a family organization of some type was formed, and the transfer of some of the attributes of the family to the clan and tribe, as well as, later, to the village and city. Some evidence exists for the conjecture that some minimal effort was made to establish a division of labor among the members of the society and institutions to support it. One of these supports seems to have been magical practices used in the hunt and in the need of the social group to bond together as a unit. It is logical to suppose, although it cannot be proven, that this includes the primitive form of magic and superstition found among the Stone Age tribes that still exist today. From these analogies it can also be conjectured that it included some type of spiritual animism, i.e., the attribution of spirit of some type to all objects whether animate or inanimate. If this were accurate it would also lead to the theory that they had some type of structure that would support a view of good and evil actions in the spirits that inhabited these objects. The burial practices would indicate that they also had a well-developed concept of the after life. Whether or not they had begun to use a pantheon of gods and goddesses that were attached to specific natural phenomena is unknown; however, the practices of stone-age people who exist today offer evidence that this practice may have existed even at this time.

All of this has to be explained in some manner by both those who advocate religion and those who advocate atheism. Many of these practices, in a much more developed form, can be found in the foundations of all modern religions. The advocates of religion, if they wish to be consistent, would have to attribute this process of development to god. Primitive man may have been in contact with god through the use of magic, or through some type of superstitious practice; the point is that god must have revealed his plan to primitive man in a manner open to his understanding. At the very least the idea of religion (the supernatural) had to be revealed to primitive man by god in some manner.

Atheism, on the other hand, would only point to the fact that it is a natural development of human need to create the institutions and practices that answer to that need. The hunt was the main support of the social unit and it is only natural that man would use magic and superstition to shape the organization and conduct of the hunt into as effective a process as possible. This is one possible way of interpreting the cave drawings found in southern France. The concern for the dead (primitive ancestor worship?) may be the rationale behind the creation of the concept of the after life (social bonding).

The point is that, whether the process was part of god's plan revealed to mankind, or a natural process dependent upon the use of human reason without the benefit of divine intervention — the archeological record clearly shows that the process occurred over a period of some 20,000 years or so. This would clearly indicate that taken as a whole the process was a slow evolution of ideas and techniques. It is true that some religious advocates accept the theory of evolution as set forth by modern science and incorporate it into their theology. In doing so, however, they must either explain or give up the concept of the Garden of Eden and other religious tenets as myth or allegory. Atheism is only required to accept evolution as a natural process and to demand that the theory be applied to explain the archeological facts as they exist.

Due to the large gaps that exist in the archeological record for this period of time, much of what passes as scientific "truth" is mere conjecture. In many cases the facts, as they exist, do not support these theories without the incorporation of other sources of information. Most of this support comes from the use of analogy, i.e., taking the facts gathered from the observation of primitive tribes that exist today and applying them to the hypothetical life of earlier mankind. This same technique is applied to the earliest known written records, that is to say, the practices that exist at the time of the earliest writings are assumed to have undergone a long period of development prior to being written down. These techniques, while they can be accepted, must be accepted only tentatively, as they may not represent an accurate picture of earlier practices. The concept of primitive man developing the foundations of civilization and society through the revealed word of god, however, is not supported by either the facts or the use of

28

analogy. It is here, at the very beginning, that we find the division between what we take on faith alone and what we take as valid conjecture based upon the facts as they exist.

In summary, we can see from the earliest archeological records available that mankind was attempting to solve some very basic problems. He was first of all faced with the enormous problem of obtaining and using a variety of food sources to insure his survival. It can safely be assumed that most, if not all, of his time and effort went into addressing this one problem. In connection with this basic level of existence, hunting large animals and gathering fruits, etc., social organization was very minimal. What social interaction there was is thought to have revolved around the nuclear family, or possibly the extended family or troop. Whatever the form of organization, it is believed at this time to have been largely instinctual and not the result of planning. The archeological record of this period also does not support any suppositions that the groups evidenced any concern with the division of labor among the members or any class organization other than the possible deference to a dominant male. There is not even any evidence to support the conjecture that Neanderthal used any type of organized hunting techniques. What the archeological does show is that Neanderthal was capable of making a variety of tools used in the hunt, and the burial of the dead in an apparently intentional manner. It is pure conjecture from these types of archeological finds that Neanderthal had at least a rudimentary belief in the supernatural and the ability to use a primitive division of labor and organized hunting techniques. Whatever the true position of Neanderthal was it is now essentially lost to us unless new finds give us more facts to base our decisions upon.

The next stage of the archeological record clearly shows that man had attained a higher level of ability in reorganizing the data of his environment into more complex structures of thought. The food sources had been extended beyond game animals and wild fruits, nuts and berries to the point at which he began to depend upon the domestication of plants and animals as a major source of his survival, at least in the area of the Near East. The transition to this new food source required the development of new methods of social organization, spurred on by the need for greater effort and greater numbers of workers to produce this food. The archeological record clearly indicates a steady growth of permanent villages of greater and greater size. The accumulation of greater numbers of people in closer association with one another also brought the need to develop new social skills. The archeological record clearly shows evidence of the use of the concept of a division of labor (the creation of specialized functions for individuals), and the development of a primitive form of government.

It can be conjectured that mankind had also developed some method of bonding the members of the village into a homogenous group. From the later written record it is surmised that this bonding agent was religion. These conjectures are not supported by the actual archeological record but the use of analogy from the written records that appeared in the area at a later date make these conjectures almost certain. The fact remains that mankind, at least in the Near East, was now living in much larger groupings, was producing a wider diversity of tools, and had begun to alter the plants and animals that existed in his environment through domestication and planned control. For whatever reason, mankind was now involved in the planned alteration of his environment and clearly he developed the techniques needed to effect this change. At this stage, the atheistic position need only accept the facts as they are and point out that the lifestyle associated with these changes would necessarily have been more complex also. The position of religion on this matter must be somewhat different. It must, under the demands of its system of beliefs, show how the supernatural enters into the development of mankind. Religion should show how and why the supernatural extended the knowledge that supported the new lifestyle, i.e., the domestication of wild plants and animals, and how that fits into the divine plan as set forth in the books of the faith.

As we shall see later, the first attempt to explain the existence of government, social structures, work, and many other processes was to create a myth around which the supernatural delivered these "goods" to mankind fully developed. One such belief, in the form of a story, is the Christian belief that God created man in his own image, including the skills and intellect that would enable him to master all the skills, processes and systems that existed at the time, i.e., the skill of farming and herding, the use of government, the creation of various social structures. As we shall see, this approach no longer holds up if one accepts the definition of what is rational, as set forth in the Introduction.

At any rate, we now have reached the point at which we do not need to rest exclusively on the archeological record for our facts. We now also have the extant written records of the cultures that existed some 7,000 years ago in the Near East and in Egypt.

Chapter 2. The Early Written Records

With the advent of written records around 6,500 years ago, in the Near East, the position of both religion and atheism no longer need to base themselves on the archeological record and analogy as the sole source of our knowledge. But prior to the development of writing, no direct evidence was left that might tell us just what religious practices were in use. Therefore we can only use a vague term like "primitive religion" to designate the religious practices (if any) that may have been common in that era. Primitive religion would include superstition, magic and an array of gods and goddesses associated with natural phenomena. These gods and goddesses were cast in human form and behaved like human beings: They were capable of human emotions such as anger, hatred, love, etc. Superstition largely revolved around the concept of the taboo. Each action was seen to be either beneficial or harmful to mankind. The actions that were harmful were considered to be taboo and were not to be committed. The actions that were beneficial were incorporated into the religion by creating a god or goddess to represent them and by worshipping these actions. Magic may be seen as the actual ritual used by man to influence the actions of the gods and goddesses or even the actions of individual living persons. In addition each aspect of nature — trees, natural springs, and streams — was seen to have its own spiritual existence. This came to be known as animism and may have been the earliest type of religious practice.

As we shall see, the major natural phenomena all came to be worshipped through the establishment of gods and goddesses. Each people seem to have worshipped some aspect of nature in preference to others, but some were common to all men, such as the wind, the sun, the moon and the rain. This was particularly true of agricultural societies. It is also likely that an oral tradition consisting of mythological stories was passed down from generation to generation, explaining the gods and goddesses and their attributes. It is this oral tradition that was later written down and became the basis of all religions.

This type of religion can certainly be found in all of the earliest written records of the agricultural peoples of the Near East. These cultures established what has come to be known as official state religions. In many ways, they do not differ much from those that exist today. For example, the earliest written records show that religion in these areas had already progressed to the point where a priesthood had been created to interpret the mythology and to establish the correct ritual to be used in worship. In short, they had already become the official keepers of the true religion.

The earliest of these cultures were the Sumerians, who were located in what is now southern Iraq, and the Egyptians. Although there is some evidence of early contact between these two cultures it is believed that they developed independently. The form of writing used and the language that supported the writing were so different that most scholars rule out the possibility that they had any substantial amount of contact. The Egyptian and Sumerian languages do not even belong to the same language family, and that indicates that they underwent thousands of years of separate development. The fact that the actual civilizations they created were fundamentally different in structure and content would also indicate that they were essentially independent of contact with each other during the few centuries of development just prior to the creation of writing. If the art of writing was a common inheritance, the source of this inheritance is now completely lost to history. What is important for our purposes is that the two societies have left us extensive written records that have allowed us to piece together the story of how they lived, and in particular, to take a good look at their religious practices.

There are several important issues that arise in the written records of these two cultures in relation to religion in general. From the knowledge that we have today, it would be safe to say that they represent the first organized states that both covered a large extent of territory and also included a wide diversity of peoples. Prior to the development of writing, it appears that mankind's social organization had not gone much beyond what was necessary to maintain the tribal and village structure. In the village-type structure, the people seem to have been closely related in terms of their language, physical features and customs. They may or may not have shared these attributes with the villages that lay close by them. It does appear, however, that there was a large degree of homogeneity or similarity throughout the Near East at this time, while a larger degree of diversity existed in northeast Africa. It is certain that the peoples who occupied a large portion of the Near East spoke languages that were of a different family from those that were spoken in Africa. It is also believed that there may have been a third language family, centered in the area of modern Turkey and northern Syria. It is also apparent that the Near East displayed many distinct customs, religious beliefs and social organizations different from those which existed in Africa (and, possibly, from those in the more northern portions of the Near East). As stated above, while mankind was evolving more complex systems for organizing the material world that surrounded him, the pattern of his thought was also becoming more complex. The written records of the Sumerians and the Egyptians make it clear that mankind had achieved a very high level of complexity in his social, political, emotional and intellectual organization. Few aspects of the modern world cannot be traced back in their origin to one of these two societies. History clearly shows that the years that separate the modern world and that of these two societies is a story of continual development of common ideals. It must be understood that, at the time the Sumerians and Egyptians developed writing, what they wrote about only affected a small proportion of the people who were contained in the culture. The records clearly show that there was a wide separation between the people who were educated and those who were not — the former being the rulers, in every branch of life, and the latter being the workers who supported them. The writings concentrate almost exclusively on the ruling and educated classes, except for an occasional derogatory remark about the lesser members of society. For example, it is believed that the vast majority of people, although they may have been aware of the state religion, and may even have participated in the rituals and ceremonies, continued to practice older forms of superstition and magic. People at all social levels were included in various forms of large-scale social organization and control. A very high percentage of the population participated in major projects such as pyramid building, road building and the maintenance of irrigation systems to benefit the society as a whole. However, when one sorts through the written records of these peoples, the writing most often refers not to the whole society but rather to the lives and concerns of the select few.

Each village or collection of villages is thought to have been developing in relative isolation to the others. This led to each having its own suite of gods and goddesses, customary ritual practice and social organization. The evolution of larger political organizations, such as those represented by the Sumerians and the Egyptians, required a new pattern of social and religious organization. Both of these states incorporated large territories that contained several major cities and innumerable villages. As the two states developed, they were forced to deal with a large number of diverse customs, languages, social structures and religious practices. As they incorporated these varying lifestyles they were also required to create a system under which all could be induced to participate in the larger social organization. Both cultures seem to have responded to this need by creating a well-organized state religion.

The records show that both cultures took the same approach, that is, as far as possible they incorporated the major gods and goddesses, customary ritual practices and superstitions that existed into the new state religion. The pantheons of both state religions were extensive, as were the ritual practices and mythology that supported them. In the case of Egypt, this practice went so far that when the two cultures of the north and south were united (to form what became the powerful state that we think of as ancient Egypt), the leading deities of each area shared the honor of supreme god. As a result, the state religions were composed of a large number of deities, ritual customs and mythological stories (theology).

In support of the state religion, both Sumer and Egypt also created a large class of people whose sole function within the society was the development and indoctrination of the people into the combined beliefs of the new Empire. This class, generally known as the priesthood, rapidly became a very powerful factor in both cultures. As a means of accomplishing their task the priesthood took what had always been a personal experience and converted it to one of an abstract nature. In order to bridge this gap both cultures took the same approach: The rulers, not the individuals, were said to have personal contact with the deities. In Egypt the ruler was considered, literally, to be the god in a human form. In Sumer, although the ruler seems not to have been considered divine in his own person, he was seen as the personal representative of the deity chosen to rule over the people.

Over time, both cultures also evolved elaborate rituals and methods of sacrifice in connection with the worship of the ruler or the state itself. This is the first record we have of the incorporation of religion as the main support for the secular government. In both cultures, specific times and places were designated for the public practice of these rituals and sacrifices. The state sponsored these festivals and the people were fed and cared for at the public expense. They were also treated to an elaborate display of the wealth and power of the state as the representative of the deity. As part of the show of wealth, great temples were constructed to display the power of the state and the deity. These temples were held out to be the actual residence of the deity in question, and were sacred in their own right. Smaller temples were constructed throughout the territory that was under the control of the two cultures; the temples honored both the major state deities and those of more local importance. As a result, the majority of the people were put into daily contact with both the state and the religion which supported it.

The duration of these two cultures testifies to the effectiveness of the systems created. It is of interest to note that one of the major problems faced by both Sumer and Egypt was the conflict between the power of the secular government and the power of the priesthood. In many ways this problem has not been solved to this day.

From the very beginning of the written record, it is clear that the priesthood had secured the status of an almost independent power within the state. In some periods they were actually in day-to-day control of the state and in other periods they were strongly under the control of the secular government. In either case, however, they were always the major moral and ethical support of the secular state. The records of both states clearly show that the evolution of the secular social organization into larger more complex systems was paralleled by the growth of larger and more complex systems of religion. By outlining the various aspects of the systems we can understand the current state of both the secular and religious organizations that exist today.

We will look at each culture separately, as they evolved along somewhat different lines. The Sumerian culture was spread over several major cities, each apparently independent of the others to a very large degree. Each city had a number of villages that were included within its recognized area of control. Each city had its own king and ruling class, as well as a chief priest; each city also seems to have had its own gods and goddesses as well as rituals to go with them. Throughout most of Sumerian history, these cities existed without defensive walls; that is a strong sign that peaceful conditions existed between them. In Sumer, therefore, the official state religion was not so strongly based on the sharing of a common pantheon of deities and ritual as it was in Egypt. Accordingly, the priesthood also seems to have been organized on a smaller, less complex basis and the priests held much less power than in Egypt. According to written records that have been discovered, all that Sumer held in common was a set of mythological stories, a common religious architecture and a common ethical heritage. The center of Sumerian religion was located in the large independent cities. It was here that the king — as the personal representative of the deity that owned the city — lived, as well as the chief priest and his immediate staff. The king had his appointed representatives in each village attached to the capital, and the chief priest also had his representatives in the villages. In the case of the king, the representatives were assigned the duties of making sure that the taxes were collected, that grain was distributed as needed, that the natural resources were mined and exploited appropriately, and the secular government furnished with men to serve as soldiers and other functionaries. In the case of religion, the duty was to teach and inculcate the village population to be loyal to the gods and to the secular government. As a matter of fact, the only separation between the secular government and the official state religion was the duties assigned to each. The system worked: these cultures were strong and long lasting, 2,000 years or so in the case of the Sumerians and 5,000 years or so in the case of Egypt. That clearly shows the flexibility and success of these systems. Although the average person was still tightly bound to the practices of ancient superstition and magic, the road had been built that leads to modern religion.

There are a few hints in the written records of this time that at least the educated members of society expressed a great deal of skepticism towards the superstitions and magic of the common people, but it appears that the skepticism of the upper classes had little or no effect on the society generally. There is no evidence that any of them, including the elite, were atheistic.

The mythological foundation of the official state religion of the Sumerian culture is directly relevant to religions that developed later. The Sumerians had a mythological story that set forth the facts of a great flood, with a single man chosen by the gods of Sumer to build an ark and take upon it representatives of all the living creatures. The story differs very little from that which can be found in the modern Christian Bible. Modern science now suggests that, due to a geological development, the Black Sea was flooded very suddenly by the Mediterranean Sea, perhaps as recently as 7,000 years ago — in other words, within the memory of modern man. If this hypothesis is accurate, then it is no wonder that such an event should be included in the written records of the Sumerians some 500 years later. Among other mythological stories contained within the Sumerian tradition is the story of the Garden of Eden. In the Sumerian story, the gods created an area in which the first man was placed, and he was provided with everything that he could want or need. This first man succumbed to temptation to eat from the Tree of Life, and was condemned to die, as was every generation of mankind from that time onward. Again, the story as related in Sumerian writings differs very little from that found in the modern Christian Bible. There are also stories that concern the delights of heaven and the torments of hell, and others narrating the creation and many other subjects treated in the modern Christian Bible. These stories come from cultures and societies that existed before the Old Testament was written. The basic mythological beliefs of the three major religions of the Near East (in the historical order in which they appeared: Judaism, Christianity, and Islam), can be traced directly back to the culture of the ancient Sumerians. This is important support for atheists.

It is also of important to note that by 2500 BC[1] the written records of the Sumerians begin to mention the fact that they were beginning to build defensive walls. This in itself would indicate that they either had reached a point at which the various city-states were warring among themselves, or that alien peoples were invading them. We have additional information: that external factors, found in the history of the wider region, were coming into play. The Sumerian culture was suffering from the wholesale migration of an alien people into their region. In a very short time, a new language family replaced the Sumerian language. (The Sumerian language is related to no other known language family now in existence.) The language family that replaced the Sumerian language is clearly Semitic in family affiliation and was related directly to those that are now used in the Near East. As a result of the migration of these alien peoples, all knowledge of the Sumerians, as an independent cultural phenomenon, was lost to the memory of mankind until very recent times. Apparently, the Sumerians were overrun, and replaced by a wholesale migration of peoples over a relatively short period of time. It is obvious, however, that the new peoples adopted at least two aspects of the Sumerian culture: the art of writing and the mythological foundations of their religion.

Although both Sumer and Egypt adopted the same general pattern to solve the problems of social and religious evolution, there were major differences.

---

1. All dates will now appear in the conventional notations of BC and AD for the convenience of the reader. The author regrets the use of these time references and their relationship to a religious personage, but it is a standard convention. For those who may not know, BC represents time before Christ, and AD represents time after the death of Christ.

While the populations that made up the Sumerian culture appear to have been relatively homogenous, the populations that made up the original Egyptian Empire consisted of at least two unrelated peoples. The earliest writings of the Egyptians describe the events that surround the unification of two separate kingdoms into a consolidated empire. It would be safe to assume that the Northern Kingdom was much more closely related to the other peoples of the Near East. The Southern Kingdom seems to have been more closely related to the peoples who occupied what are now modern Sudan and Ethiopia. The language of the ancient Egyptians seems to be related to the languages currently used in these two areas, and that fact has led scholars to associate the Southern Kingdom with Sudan and Ethiopia. As a result of the diversity of lifestyles and customs between the two kingdoms, Egypt from the very beginning had to establish a much more extensive and aggressive secular government. This in turn seems to have generated the need for a much more organized and aggressive state religion than that of Sumer. This was true at every level for both the secular government and the state religion, according to written evidence that has come to light through the efforts of modern archeology. In Egypt, for example, the Pharaoh was not only the appointed representative of the divine on earth but was in fact considered the divine, in human form.

Egyptian society, at the highest levels, was divided into two different systems of power. At one level, the secular, power was centered on the Pharaoh's immediate family members, who shared in his divinity. Then there was the relatively independent priesthood, which was not apparently considered to be divine in form — although they were treated as divine, in fact. In Egypt, the day-to day operations of the secular government were conducted by both the secular and religious arms to a much greater degree than in Sumer. In the Egyptian culture, it is very difficult to mark the actual line of demarcation between the religious and the secular organizations.

The religion created by the Egyptians was by the nature of their social system much more organized and disciplined than that of Sumer. As a consequence, religion played a much larger role in the day-to-day life of Egypt. The common person, from the highest-ranking professionals, such as the royal architects, scribes, priests and others, to the common farmer all had to devote a large portion of their time to state projects. At times, whole peoples would be captured and brought to Egypt as workmen for the state. This seems to have been the case with the ancient Hebrews. As a result of such practices the theology, pantheon of deities, and rituals of the state religion were more numerous and diverse than any other to be found at that time in the ancient world. It is difficult to find a god or goddess, a religious belief or ritual in either the later Near East or Europe that was not also found in Egypt. In most cases the beliefs, deities and rituals that were brought to Egypt by the captured peoples were merely incorporated into the state religion. This helped ease the assimilation of new peoples into the Egyptian system. In other cases, as with the later Hebrews, the beliefs were merely tolerated by the Egyptians and became religious cults operating within the broader state religion. As time went by, the state religion (or the cults) came to include all of the later beliefs that are to be found in Judaism, Christianity and Islam with the exception of the concept of monotheism and the spiritual nature of the deity. The taboos found in extant writings include prohibitions against the eating of pork and the drinking of wine, as well as injunctions to cover the head in the presence of what is holy, and the seclusion of women. In addition to these taboos and injunctions there were cults that expressed a belief in prophecy, redemption by a personal savior, and virgin birth.

The Egyptians also were the first to create a system within the state religion that would today be recognized as a Church. The Egyptian church was based upon a complex theology concerned with the problem of death. Everyone is aware of the Egyptians' concern with the preservation of the rulers through the construction of pyramids and mummification; the same principles, on a much less grand scale, were also a part of the day-to-day concerns of the common people. In many ways the Egyptian Book of the Dead can be seen as the precursor of later books of religion, such as the Bible.

It can be stated without much question that a large share of the content of the three modern Near Eastern religions, i.e., Judaism, Christianity and Islam, is based upon the beliefs of Sumer and Egypt as we now know them. The two concepts that can be found in the modern religions that do not appear in either Sumer or Egypt are the concepts of monotheism and incorporeal spirituality. There was one abortive attempt in Egypt to establish the concept of monotheism under the ruler Akhnaton, but this proved to be short lived. We shall follow the development of these two concepts in the next chapter, when we deal with the later religions of the area. The concept of true spirituality is also alien to both of the cultures. They do not seem to have contemplated the idea of a deity who had no substance of any form and who was omnipotent and omnipresent. In both Sumer and Egypt, the divine was seen as having a form which would allow men to not only see the deities but to actually communicate with them. In both cultures, a deity might routinely take on human form and react as a human would react. In short, in both cultures the divine was capable of being known and understood by human reason. This was altered, later, into a divine concept that was unknowable and not capable of being understood by man. Again, this development will be followed in detail in the next chapter.

The remainder of this chapter will be devoted to following the patterns by which the ideas contained in the Sumerian and Egyptian cultures spread throughout the Near East and Europe.

Outside the actual territory controlled by these two cultures, it appears from the written and archeological records that a very homogenous culture existed. Initially, the area comprised by the modern Near East, including modern Turkey, was occupied by peoples who spoke languages in the Semitic language family, or, in the case of northern Iran, peoples who spoke a language related directly to that of Sumer. It seems that there were two major lifestyles to be found in this region. The majority of the population seems to have been occupied in the two major types of farming, in other words, the herding of domesticated animals or the growing of crops. The rest of the population seems to have been occupied in the business of trade, particularly when we talk about the people who occupied the coastline cities of the Red Sea and the Mediterranean. Large centers were established in the interior that conducted trading activities through the use of caravans. In both cases, the peoples that conducted trade were largely involved in gathering the raw materials produced by the interior peoples and exchanging them for the finished products of the urban civilizations. The archeological record, in particular, clearly shows that the finished products of both Sumer and Egypt can be found throughout the Near East, northern Africa, the islands of the Mediterranean, southern and southeastern Europe and as far away as Central Asia and India. The Sumerians do not appear to have been a seafaring people and little or no mention is made in their written records of caravan activities. The Egyptians of the Old Kingdom do appear to have had a large commercial navy and created the first canal system between the Red and Mediterranean seas. The bulk of their naval activity, however, seems to have been concentrated on the southeastern coastline of the Red Sea, connecting them with eastern Africa, the western and southern coasts of Arabia, and the eastern Mediterranean. On the other hand, the raw materials that found their way to the urban cultures can be traced to the interior of Europe, all the way to the Baltic Sea area, and as far to the east as southern Russia and Central Asia. The archeological record of the urban cultures shows amber that can only be found in the vicinity of the Baltic Sea and semi-precious stones that are found only in Central Asia. It is generally believed that the naval activities of the coastal peoples and the caravans of the interior carried the raw materials that found their way to the urban centers from these areas. In return, these same peoples carried the finished products of the urban cultures back to the peoples living throughout Europe, the Near East and Central Asia. The importance, for our discussion, of the existence of long-established trade routes throughout this area is that it led to the transmission of the cultural attributes of the two urban civilizations to a wide area and a diverse range of peoples. It is very likely that the constant contact of the trading peoples with those of the urban cultures resulted in a large amount of intermarriage between them. This in turn facilitated the incorporation of the techniques of the fine arts, and the thought and the religious ideas of the urban cultures into that of the trading peoples, and vice versa. These, in turn, were carried further by the trading peoples, who can also be assumed to have intermarried with the peoples who provided the raw material as their contribution to the trade system. Through this network of contacts and exchanges, the art of writing, the mythological stories, and the religious and philosophical thought of the urban peoples were slowly spread across the whole area. It is of particular importance here to mention again the relatively peaceful conditions that seem to have been the rule across this area from about 4500 BC, until roughly 2500 BC.

As a matter of convenience, scholars give the general designation of "Indo-European" to the migrating peoples. The term denotes the fact that although many different dialects were spoken, all of the languages appear to have belonged to the same language family. It also denotes the large degree of similarity between the customs, lifestyle and technology of all of the various peoples who make up this designation. There is still some confusion concerning the connection between the earliest immigrants and those who came later. The original migration which seems to have occurred around 2500 BC and which seems to have been initiated in the Black and Caspian Sea basins; and to have affected mainly northern and central Turkey, as well as northern Iran. The best known of the peoples who migrated at this time are the Hyksos and the Hittites. Both seem to have moved into northern and central Turkey. In the process, they seem to have pushed the peoples who occupied these areas further south. Included in this forced migration, it seems, were the Phoenicians and the Akkadians. It is also thought, although less well documented, that the Mitanni moved into northern Iran at about the same time, destroying the almost unknown culture of that area. The affiliation of the Hyksos, Hittite and Mittanni peoples with those generally classified as Indo-European is doubtful. The languages spoken by these peoples show some resemblance to other Indo-European languages, but are far enough removed to also be considered as a separate language family. As a result, they are sometimes classified as proto Indo-European. The archeological and written records available show a clear picture of the change that was beginning to appear at about 2500 BC. The most salient aspect of this period is the large migrations of peoples beginning about 2500 BC and ending about 800 BC. Initially, the migrations seem to have affected the areas now known as modern Turkey and the coastlines of modern Lebanon and Syria. It is believed that these migrations were induced by the continued alteration of the climate of Central Asia and the grasslands of Eastern Europe. The climate had been slowly changing from one that was warmer and wetter than the climate that exists today. As the climate became colder and dryer, the dense grasslands became much sparser and supported fewer animals and crops. This in turn appears to have created a period of serious over-population across the whole area. The over-population seems to have led to the wholesale migration of entire peoples into new areas of habitation. Generally, this migration was directed towards the south, where there was a perception of plenty generated by the trading activities and the knowledge gained from them by the migrating peoples.

These earlier migrations seem to have had several major effects on the urban cultures of the south. They brought with them some advancement in technology including the art of working iron. This had allowed them to develop weapons that were much superior to those used by the Sumerians or Egyptians.

In addition, they seem to have brought the first war chariots into the area, which provided them with a vast tactical superiority. These military advantages seem to have been adopted by the people whom they forced out of the area. As these peoples moved further south, the result was the complete destruction of the Sumerian culture and the related culture that existed at that time in northern Iraq. The destruction of these cultures was so complete that their very existence — even in the memory of mankind — was lost until modern times. Further west, the Hyksos continued their drive southward and eventually overthrew the Old Kingdom dynasty of Egypt. They did not, however, seem to have any affect upon the underlying culture of Egypt. The original period of migration seems to have ended around 1800 BC, with the return of relatively peaceful times.

The archeological and written records would seem to indicate that the urban cultures of Sumer and the areas related to it were essentially alien to the Semitic peoples who surrounded them. The peaceful period which followed the first migrations saw the complete absorption and adaptation of the urban cultures by the new Semitic peoples into a distinctive culture of their own. Further west and north, the new peoples seem to have had a much closer relationship with the Egyptians than with the Semitic peoples. The same seems to be true of the Semitic peoples who occupied the coastlines of the Red Sea. In this area, the Egyptians, for various periods of time, had direct military control.

This state of affairs seems to have lasted until about 1500 BC, when a new set of migrations began which involved the true Indo-Europeans. These later migrations seem to have been periodic in nature and to have lasted until roughly 800 BC. The earliest of these migrations seems to have been concentrated in the area of modern Afghanistan and Northwestern India. The peoples involved have been given the designation of Vedic (also Indo-Aryan) in connection with their earliest writings, the Vedas. These peoples came into contact with the urban cultures that had evolved in northwestern India and the Indus valley of Pakistan. We do not know much about these urban cultures, except that they did have a system of writing and had developed a high degree of material culture. The Vedic peoples adapted their system of writing to their own language, producing ancient Sanskrit. The blending of the culture of the Vedic peoples and urban cultures of India led over a period of some 700 years to the development of the religion of Hinduism. This later led to the evolution of another great modern religion, Buddhism. It is unknown how much effect this process of consolidation in India had on the cultures that had been established in Central Asia and in particular that which had developed in Afghanistan.

The Near East and Egypt seem to have been largely unaffected by this second wave of migrations, allowing an additional period of consolidation to occur. The records indicate that the main lines of this consolidation period were greatly influenced by Egypt. The cultures that occupied the interior of the Near East had adapted the mythology and technology of the Sumerians to their own use but had, in essence, lost any direct line of influence with that culture. The secular system that had been established in Old Kingdom Egypt seems to have had the greatest influence on the area. Their use of the empire system was adopted over the whole area. The rulers were seen to be divine in their person in the same manner as the pharaoh of Egypt. They also adopted the Egyptian use of a well-organized and disciplined priesthood supported by an equally well-organized and disciplined military aristocracy. These adoptions from the Egyptian culture were then modified to fit the needs of the Semitic peoples. The priesthood soon developed well-thought-out and complete theologies to support the state religions. The religions themselves were even more closely related and married to the secular government. In short, they developed what we would easily recognize as organized religion today. The marriage of the secular government to religion was extended to include the divine sanction of the secular laws by which the people were ruled. The tenets of the various religions were quickly written down and soon became immutable. They were then extended to encompass the day-to-day behavior of the people as a standard of moral and ethical conduct. In short, the system developed in the Near East came to be involved in every aspect of the daily life of the people. At the same time, the many individual religious cults that existed throughout the area seem to have been largely tolerated by the governments, as they did not pose a direct threat to them.

About 1100 BC, another series of migrations took place affecting mostly the areas now contained in northwest Turkey and southeastern Europe. In these areas a group of Indo-European peoples, who later become known collectively as Greeks, began to occupy the northwestern portions of Turkey, especially the coastline along the Mediterranean. They also settled in the area of southeastern Europe known as the Balkans. It is unknown whether or not they absorbed the earlier peoples who had made up the Hittite culture, but it is likely that they at least adopted and adapted a great degree of that culture to their own use. These adoptions most likely included the art of writing and many of the technological achievements associated with the Hittites.

Over a period of some 300 years, this branch of the migrations settled into two major areas of influence, the coastline of northwestern Turkey and the mainland of Greece. The earliest to develop was that located in modern Turkey, which produced the culture that appears around 800 BC in the tales of Homer concerning the city of Troy. The later culture, which has become the best known of the Greek civilizations, developed between 800 BC and 500 BC. It is interesting that the development of this portion of the Greek culture seems to have been essentially independent of contact with the Near East and Egypt, except through their contact with the Greeks who lived in Turkey.

The civilization developed was therefore quite different in almost all aspects from that which had evolved in the Near East and Egypt. Some of the most important differences can be summarized as follows. The Greeks from the beginning seem to have taken great pains to separate the concept of religion from that of secular life. They did attribute the creation of the idea of government, the arts, technology and most attributes of life to the supernatural. Once created or given to mankind, however, the Greeks believed that it was the responsibility of mankind to develop and use these gifts. This development and use was to be governed solely by man using his own reason. The rulers were not seen to be divine in their person and were not even the representative of the divine on earth. They were instead elected by the military aristocracy and held power only at the tolerance of this aristocracy. Initially, the Greeks do not appear to have had an organized religion but relied on a very primitive set of beliefs. These were based on animism, that is, the belief that each object (whether animate or inanimate) had a spiritual existence as well as its material existence. They also had developed a pantheon of gods and goddesses that were associated mostly with natural phenomena. These latter had been construed to appear in human form and were saddled with most of the human attributes. In fact, the main difference between the deities and humans was the fact that the deities were immortal and had much greater power. The gods and goddesses were even seen to be capable of mating with humans and producing offspring that were semi-divine. Such a being was the famous Hercules. For the Greeks, the supernatural was not some unknown or unknowable being but rather a form of existence that could be totally understood by the use of human reason.

Toward the end of this period of development, another branch of the Indo-European peoples seem to have migrated into northern Iran. We do not know where this people came from, but it is assumed that they migrated from either the eastern shores of the Caspian Sea or from southwestern Afghanistan. They became known to history as the Persians. They seem to have had many traits in common with the ancient Greeks, at first; but soon, through their close contact with the Semitic peoples, especially those of the urban culture known as Assyria, they adopted ways more closely associated with the Near East. They do not represent a direct influence on the evolution of Western European civilization and will be handled separately in the next chapter in relation to their influence on Islam.

As a general rule the religion, as well as the lifestyle, of the Indo-Europeans seems to have been very practical in nature. As a result, their art tended to be very realistic, including their portrayal of the supernatural. Their thought also tended to be very much based upon the use of human reason and therefore tends to be rational in content. This can be seen clearly in the modern tendency to see the Indo-European religions as schools of philosophy rather than as developed theologies. These two tendencies contain the main explanations for the vast difference in approach between them and the peoples of the Near East and Egypt in relation to religion. The effect of the Greek culture on the evolution of Western European civilization cannot be overstated. This would include its influence on what today we would call the atheistic philosophy, which is the main interest of this work. It is generally agreed that the Greek culture was the most rational of any of the ancient cultures.

It must be stated, however, that even in Greece itself the involvement of the Greeks with the evolution of human reason affected only a small minority of the total population. The Greek culture was limited to a large degree to the upper classes of the various city-states, just as writing and the higher attainments of culture had been restricted in Sumer. The majority of the population was uneducated and was locked into beliefs that included mostly superstition and magic. The Greeks did develop a well-organized state religion but the upper classes, at least, exercised a high degree of skepticism in relation to it. The official religion, as stated earlier, consisted of a pantheon of gods and goddesses associated with the various natural phenomena, coupled with a rather elaborate mythology and ritual to explain their functions in relation to human beings. These latter seem to be blatantly aimed at creating an atmosphere among the people that ought to lead to the production of good citizens. Each city-state seems to have had its own patron god or goddess and a supporting mythology concerning its foundation. It is remarkable how closely the state religion of the Greeks resembles that of Sumer, although it is accepted that the Greeks could not have known of the Sumerians. As time went on, contact with the peoples of the Near East and Egypt increased and the various cults that existed in these areas began to seep into Greece proper and became mixed with the more primitive superstition of the Greeks.

What is truly unique to the Greeks is their development of what we call today philosophy. Two separate developments of Greek philosophy were still clear in its later history. One branch of Greek philosophy was centered in the cities that dotted the Mediterranean coast of western Turkey; the other was based on the mainland of Greece itself. Although both branches of the Greek world remained in constant contact with each other, the two main lines of philosophical thought appear to have evolved independently. It is likely that the branch that developed in Turkey was in earlier contact with the thought of the Near East, especially that of Persia and Egypt, and on a larger scale, than were the Greeks of the mainland. It also appears that the mainland Greeks were in close contact with the civilization that occupied the island of Crete and that came to be called the Minoan civilization.

Regardless of the source of the differences in philosophical temperament, the result was two divergent lines of philosophical thought by about 600 BC. The Greeks who occupied the coastline of Turkey very early in their history began to develop what today we would call science. They based their system on what has become known today as the philosophy of materialism. This system set forth the belief that the universe was composed solely of natural elements. As a result, they dismissed the supernatural as a cause of the universe. They believed that the universe was initially composed of one substance that existed as an undifferentiated unity. This substance was seen as being eternal and uncreated. This unity was variously described but can be understood generally as a complete abstraction of the concept of being. Man's place in the universe consisted not only of his participation in being but also in his ability to understand the concept of abstracted being through the use of human reason. The systems constructed around this basic foundation all were an attempt to explain the universe in terms of natural phenomena and the use of human reason. Reliance was placed on such studies as those of mathematics, astronomy, biology, chemistry and physics. These are, of course, what we today call the natural sciences. They were indeed the direct ancestors of modern science. It is also worthy of note that the general Greek disbelief in the supernatural can also be seen as the foundation of modern atheism.

The system that developed in Greece proper, although just as extensive as that of the eastern school, was more esoteric in nature. This school of thought was based upon the premise of a divine creation of the universe and all that it contains. This creation, however, did not extend to the actual objects that exist within the universe or to the physical universe itself; it was limited to the creation of the ideal archetype of the actual existing objects. This school of thought projected that there was an ideal chair, table, man and so on. From this model, the existing objects were created due to the operation of the laws of nature in all their variety, the laws of nature being seen as the active archetype created by the intellectual activity of the deity. These latter objects being merely copies of the ideal, man himself included, could be understood and used by mankind through the use of human reason. This school of thought has come to be known today as Idealism (Metaphysics). In summary, it can be stated that the two schools of thought, along with their many sub-schools, can be separated into those accepting materialism and those accepting metaphysics as their foundation.

Both schools of thought placed a high degree of reliance on human reason when considering the secular activities of man. They tried to understand the principles that served as the foundation of politics, economics, moral and ethical behavior as totally natural. The Greeks studied and wrote extensively about all of these. In the area of moral and ethical behavior, probably the best known writings are those of Plato. In the area of science, the most well known are those of Aristotle.

Let's look at one further aspect of the Greek culture. For their prosperity, the ancient Greeks depended to a large degree on commercial trading. Their two main areas of influence have already been spelled out but, in addition, through their trading activities they established colonies around the Black Sea, within the coastline cities of the Near East and Egypt, in northern Africa, on all of the Mediterranean islands and in Spain and Italy. These colonies were usually established by one of the city-states of Greece and consisted of populations actually moved to the colony from the mother city. In essence, they were enclaves of Greek citizens existing separately from the native populations of the area. As a result, the trading colonies maintained very close ties with the mother cities and shared fully in the evolving Greek civilization. The philosophers were able to freely travel throughout the areas under Greek influence and taught their systems freely. In addition, the colonies developed their own philosophers who contributed to the thought of the homeland. It is also apparent that Greek philosophers were granted a very large degree of tolerance throughout the Near East and Egypt. It is not possible today to determine how much give and take took place between the early Greek philosophies and those that existed in Crete, the Near East and Egypt. It can safely be assumed, however, that there was a considerable amount of borrowing on the part of all involved. It is likely that, at this time, however, the borrowing was greater on the part of the Greeks, as their civilization was still in the process of evolution while the Near Eastern, Egyptian, and Cretan cultures were much more solidified.

During much of the independent history of Greece, the teaching of the philosophical schools was carried on as an extensive oral tradition. It was only towards the end of the Greek period of independence that the philosophical traditions were collected into schools and written down. It is believed, however, that the writings express an accurate account of the oral tradition. These later documents represent most of the direct evidence we have concerning Greek thought and religion.

In summary, it is fair to say that by 300 BC, the major outlines of the theology, ritual and ceremony that are found in modern organized religion had already been established. These attributes had become totally ingrained in the day-to-day lives of the people of those times. The Near East and Egypt had built their cultures around the specifically religious aspects of life, even to the exclusion of any dependence on human reason beyond practical tasks.

The Greeks set forth the two major tenets that support the arguments of atheism. They were the first known people who were willing to publicly debate the existence or non-existence of the supernatural. They were also the first known people who intentionally attempted to replace religious theology with the findings of human reason. In this latter attempt, they established two main lines of argument. The first was based upon the denial of the supernatural and its replacement with a moral and ethical system of behavior based solely on human reason. The second includes an acceptance of the supernatural as the creator, but denied that it was controlling the day-to-day operation of the universe. It was here that they included the assertion that human reason was the sole means by which mankind could understand the day-to-day operation of the universe. This point appears to agree in large part with the tenets of modern agnosticism. Under agnosticism, a modern system, it is accepted that a deity exists, but the theology, ritual and ceremony of organized religion is discarded as unnecessary to the demands of day-to-day life. By contrast, the areas under Indo-European influence, particularly that of the Greeks, had become accustomed to the idea that human reason could be depended upon to answer all but the most esoteric questions. A large portion of modern history can be interpreted as the conflict between these two ways of dealing with the world around us.

The development of Greek thought as an independent phenomenon came to an end around 300 BC with the rise of the state of Macedon. Macedon was located in the region of Europe now known as the Balkans, and was a part of the Greek trading world. It does not appear, however, that Macedon was culturally a part of the Greek world — they were generally referred to as barbarians. (The word barbarian is a generalized Greek term for all non-Greek peoples, regardless of their material achievements.) Alexander the Great, the best known of the Macedonian warriors, was a pupil of Aristotle in Athens prior to his conquests. In fact, there seems to be a very high level of respect for the Greek civilization in all of Alexander's actions as well as those of his father, Phillip. During the ascendancy of Phillip, and most of that of Alexander, Greece was left free from the direct control of Macedon.

Over a period of just a few years, Alexander was able to conqueror the whole of the Near East, Egypt and southeastern Europe. His conquests reached into Central Asia and northwestern India but his forces could not consolidate their hold in these areas. At the death of Alexander, the huge empire was divided into several smaller kingdoms ruled by his major generals. The whole of the Near East and Egypt reverted almost immediately to the way of life that had existed prior to the conquest. Only in the major cities, which were the home of the Macedonian overlords, did Greek culture establish itself to any degree. Even here, the influence was no more than a very thin intellectual veneer. In Macedon proper, the Greek influence continued to support the inheritors of Alexander's throne, but the Greek city-states were unable to break free of a cycle of internal warfare, weakening themselves until they were incorporated into Macedon proper, putting an end to independent Greek civilization. Over the next 200 years, the intellectual heritage of the Greeks moved eastward to the major cities of the Near East, such as Antioch in Syria, and the to city of Alexandria in Egypt. The trading empire that had once been the glory of the Greeks was now transferred to the island state of Sicily and the Colonies located on the coast of southern Italy. This trading empire was shared by the Phoenician trading colony of Carthage that had been established in North Africa. As stated earlier, the Greek cultural influence itself had been reduced to a thin veneer throughout the Macedonian Empire.

The period of Macedonian rule has generally come to be designated as the Hellenistic era. This accurately denotes the fact that the original Macedonians were included within the Greek civilization, but also conceals the fact that the actual culture developed under the Macedonians was much more oriental than Greek. Due mainly to their continual warfare and efforts to reestablish the empire of Alexander, the Hellenes failed in their efforts to extend the achievements of Greek civilization. They contented themselves with gathering the extensive writings of the Greeks, Persians and Egyptians into vast libraries. The cities that contained these libraries became centers of scholarship and continuing commentary on the original documents, for centuries to come. This commentary is of great importance when one turns to the later development of Christianity and Islam, and will be discussed in due course. The Hellenes paid little attention to the affairs of Western Europe and interfered as little as possible with the colonies in Sicily and Italy. This allowed the development of the Etruscan and Roman peoples of northern and central Italy.

By about 100 BC, the Hellenistic impulse had spent itself on continuous warfare, luxury and waste of assets. The native cultures of the Near East and Egypt had managed to completely reassert themselves. Although they continued to be affected to some degree by Greek thought, they were not Greek in any sense of the word. In Europe, the Greek and Hellenistic civilizations were quickly swallowed by the Roman conquests. The one solid contribution of the Hellenistic world to Greek thought was the development of a school of thought known today as Neo-Platonism. This school of thought posited that the supernatural did exist, but that it was totally spiritual in nature and beyond man's power to comprehend. The tenets of organized religion were seen not as supernatural but rather as the natural development of religious thought through the use of human reason. Their aim was to control the secular activities of the government and to insure a body of loyal citizens. In short, they demanded the separation of Church and state.

Included within their concept of the supernatural was the concept that god was one, i.e., the concept of monotheism. They also believed that god acted through the word and was the word. In addition to the spiritually of the supernatural they attached the concept of the personal responsibility of the individual to know and live a moral and ethical life. This school of thought had a very strong influence on the development of the Roman state and through it the development of Christianity.

A vast amount of written heritage is included within this chapter, while the amount of time covered is short in comparison to that covered in the last chapter. It will be useful to put what has been covered in the context of the contrast between the atheistic and religious positions. During the whole period of time considered, some 6,600 years or more, religion has been evolving constantly in both its scope and in the complexity of its organization. As we have seen, it is conjectured that religion began with Neanderthal and a primitive belief in the after-life and thereby in the supernatural. By the end of this chapter, it has assumed an almost identical state with organized religion as it exists today. Atheism, on the other hand, at this point in time, either did not yet exist or existed in only its most primitive form. Atheism can be said to exist only if one considers the skepticism of the Greeks as evidence of atheistic thought. The Greek written record does indicate that the upper classes, at least, did evidence a large degree of skepticism concerning the existence of the supernatural. It also shows that the same classes ridiculed to some degree the others' belief in the god and goddesses of the Greek pantheon, especially the rituals and myth which surrounded them. The record also indicates that these classes simply did not believe in the grosser forms of magic and superstition. Many paid lip service to the official religion but did not put any real faith in it, either. Yet very few, if any, were able to take the final step and disavow a belief in the supernatural in any form. Even the segment of Greek culture which developed the so called "scientific" philosophy often admitted the efficacy of a creative force that was supernatural in form. At the very least, the Greeks believed in an abstracted form of being (nature) which they called fate and which was represented as a sort of supernatural existence. In only one way did the Greeks evidence a connection with modern atheism — and that is in their belief that the universe and all that was in it was capable of being fully understood through the use of human reason. This is not enough, however, to make the claim that atheism existed among the Greeks.

In the case of religion, a totally different picture has to be drawn. In the Near East, including western Central Asia and India, religion over the period of several millennia had evolved into a very complex system of thought and action. Over most of this area, the individual's life had become so closely bound to the theology, ritual, and duties of religious belief that religion had become essentially an instinctive behavior. No area of life was untouched by religion from birth to death — and the afterlife. For every thought and action there was a theological explanation, a ritual to perform, and an actual duty to be carried out. This had been the way, over most of the civilized world, for several thousands of years. The religious discipline was constantly inculcated into the individual's life from every direction. Very few, if any, within these societies were even capable of questioning the authority of religion. In Greece, although a few may have challenged the authority of religion, the life of the average person probably did not differ markedly from those of the Near East. Today, an atheist needs to realize that this evolution in religion occurred slowly over a relatively long period of time and that it had evolved in such a way as to seem as if it was a natural part of human nature. One does not question instincts; one does not even realize that they are in operation. One simply reacts in the way in which instinct dictates, as if there were no alternative.

As a matter of contrast, then, one can clearly postulate that, as of some 2,000 or 3,000 years ago, the atheistic position essentially did not exist and that the religious position had grown and existed for such a long period that it had become part of mankind's instinctive nature. This itself is often used by those who hold with religion to "prove" the existence of the supernatural. First, one can postulate that very early in the history of mankind, a way was found to ground the intellectual confusion that must have existed. By this, we mean that the level of complexity that had been obtained by mankind at that point was to a great degree limited to the classification of the data available, that is to say, mankind's collective knowledge was limited essentially to the "what" that existed. His knowledge did not extend to an understanding of "why" they existed or even more importantly the "how" of their existence. As a result, mankind was forced to develop a method by which these questions could be answered. The answer chosen seems to have been to remove them from their association with man and put them under the care of a supernatural being that was beyond man's understanding. It seems that man early on realized that this same supernatural power could be used to support his need for social contact and organization.

No one would question the fact that the ideas evolved in the name of religion have been one of the most powerful influences in the development of mankind. If these ideas did not develop in some such manner, then it is up to those who hold to the religious position to provide an answer that more closely fits the facts as we know them. It is at least reasonable to ask those who hold the religious position why this supernatural power did not immediately establish itself as the sole power in the formation of the universe and all that exists in it. In addition it might be asked why a perfect knowledge was not given to mankind concerning the requirements of this being from the very beginning. The religious position's best answer to these questions is merely to say that man cannot fathom the plan of the supernatural.

One further comment needs to be made at this point. Even though there is a large body of writings available for our research, it is a long way from being a complete record. It is possible that other records will be found, documents that were written at this time or somewhat later, that will completely alter our ideas of these cultures and what they believed. In addition, it must be cautioned that some of the records of contemporary cultures have not yet been deciphered, such as those of the island of Crete and northwest India (Pakistan). Once scholars find a way to decipher these writings, it is possible that they will alter the view we hold of the manner in which these ancient cultures saw their problems and their solution. Finally, all of these records were written in languages that no longer exist and must be translated into a modern language. Since they were written in a language that we no longer can learn, by persons who used thought patterns that may be totally different from ours, it is at least highly possible that they have been misunderstood in translation. This can happen either by mistranslating the actual words or by the translators' inability to recognize and override their own prejudices while apprehending someone else's thoughts and rendering them into a different language. In short, the understanding that we currently have concerning what was believed in these ancient cultures may be subject to change as we find new facts.

This brings us to the point at which it is fair to say that the modern era begins. The next chapter will go into detail concerning the development of the three modern Near Eastern religions, i.e., Judaism, Christianity and Islam. It will also follow the evolution of Christianity through the Roman Empire and its role after the fall of that empire.

CHAPTER 3. MODERN RELIGION IN THE NEAR EAST AND ROME

The Roman conquest began in the west with the consolidation of its victories over the two tribes that occupied central Italy, namely, the Etruscans and the Sabines. The consolidation was effected by granting the two tribes equal citizenship with the original Latin-speaking tribes in the foundation of the city of Rome. From this point, the Romans extended their control over the Greek colonies of southern Italy and attempted to conquer Sicily. This in turn led to a series of protracted wars against the city-state of Carthage that had been founded by the Phoenicians on the Mediterranean coast of north Africa. The Carthaginians had been able to establish a large area of control over the tribes of northern Africa and had taken control of trade in the western Mediterranean. As part of this trading empire, they had taken and maintained control of half of the island of Sicily. The Carthaginians also reached out into the Atlantic and touched the shores of Spain and France. With the victory of Rome over the Carthaginians, the Romans inherited the trade routes. It does not appear that the Romans were directly involved in trade at this time, as they did not have a commercial navy. The trade itself was still conducted by the Greeks who inhabited Sicily and their mother cities in Greece.

The social structure of the Romans consisted of a small aristocracy composed of the leading families of the tribes, a larger class of freemen composed of workmen who supported the growing industrial and agricultural activities of Rome, as well as the military. The result of the process of conquest and consolidation was the establishment of a republican form of government in Rome, which consisted of the election of the ruler by the aristocratic families of the constituent tribes. The military consisted of citizen soldiers and the social structure was already to a large extent controlled by secular law. A more detailed look at Roman social structure will be taken as we approach the point when Rome expanded into the east. During the construction of the republican form of government, Rome was able to take most of northern Italy under its control. This control extended almost to the borders of modern Switzerland. The Romans had also moved into Spain and southern France, following the trade routes established by the Carthaginians. At this time, however, these areas were not included within the citizenship structure of Rome but were established as provinces. The population of this area could, however, obtain the rights of citizenship individually either through military service or through service in the government at Rome.

By 2,000 years ago the Roman republic included all of Italy (whose inhabitants shared the right of citizenship), coupled with military and administrative control over Sicily, Spain, southern France, and North Africa (which were without the benefit of citizenship). The Greeks who inhabited the island of Sicily and the former Greek colonies of southern Italy conducted most of the Romans' trade. Relations with the Greeks of these areas brought Rome into contact with both the ancient Greek culture and that developed by the later Macedonians. The Romans adapted much of the Greek and Hellenistic culture into their own culture, including the literary, philosophical, architectural, and religious aspects. The area already under the control of the Romans was very large even by modern standards. It was soon to be made evident that the Romans had not yet reached a stage of technological development that would make it possible to govern such a large area solely under the principles of republican government. It will be of interest to follow the changes made by the Romans in their early social structure in an attempt to solve the problems of governing an empire.

The earliest history of the Romans, i.e., prior to 2,400 years ago, is largely mythological. This was the period during which the Latins were able to gain control of the Sabines and the Etruscans. It also included the original foundation of the city of Rome as an independent entity. Around 2,400 years ago, the area was invaded by the Gauls, who entered through northern Italy and so completely destroyed Rome that nothing of its written records remain and very little of its archeological record. It appears that the Etruscans were able to repel the Gauls and establish a short-lived domination over the Romans. From this point forward, developments are documented by a large amount of written records as well as a fairly complete archeological record. The records show a slow process of consolidation of the whole area under the leadership of Rome. At the same time, the Romans seem to have been in almost constant warfare with the Gauls who had taken control of northern Italy and the northern portions of France. During this period, it is also clear that Roman culture was developing largely independent of any foreign influence with the exception of the Etruscan culture. By the end of this period, the Romans had also adapted many aspects of the Carthaginian and Greek culture to its own use. The Latin language, although clearly Indo-European and therefore distantly related to the Greek language, does not seem to have been influenced in its later evolution by either Greek or Etruscan.

The clan council and the praetorian laws mitigated to some degree the abuses that developed from this legal standing of the father. Custom also seems to have softened the legal affect of this power, allowing flexibility not found in the law. One such custom was the strong sense of affection that seems to have existed between the members of the same family. The legal system was supported by a very highly developed system of ancestor worship. Christianity as it grew under Roman protection seems to have adapted many of the customary aspects of Roman family life into its theology, softening the concept of family as it was inherited and adopted from Judaism. The Romans had also developed a code of morals in relation to the family that emphasized actions that were very similar to those of the stoical school of the Greeks, and which were later adopted by the puritanical sects of Christianity. The general tenor of Roman life tended to very puritanical in nature. It tended to be very conservative in its approach to traditional knowledge, and in particular in relation to the secular law. In the area of personal morality, the Romans of this period can best be described as stoical in practice. This aspect of Roman culture also seems to have been adopted by the early Christians within the empire.

The mainstays of this early Roman culture, which continued throughout its history, had a great influence on the later development of Christianity in the West. As with most ancient cultures, the nuclear family held a position of major importance within the society. In the case of the Romans, this family unit was highly patriarchal in nature. Unlike the Jewish family that revolved around religion to the exclusion of the secular, the Roman family was closely attached to the secular social life of the Romans. By secular law, rather than by tradition, the father was the owner of his wife, the children of the marriage, the grandchildren, and the daughter-in-laws, as well as all the property of the family, no matter who earned or brought the property into the family. The father could not lose this legal right even if he attempted to give it away freely; not even if the father was insane. These absolute powers of ownership in the father were tempered somewhat by the actual practices that evolved around the family.

In religious practice, the Romans remained true to their Indo-European roots. On a day-to-day basis, they maintained the household gods and goddesses, such as Vesta (the sacred fire), which they attempted to keep burning continuously. This practice was carried into the public arena with the establishment of the Vestal virgins. Other household gods and goddesses protected the field, the home, and other family assets. Each person, and many inanimate objects, came equipped with their own personal spirit. In the case of humans, this spirit was known as Juno. The personal Juno survived the individual after death and was the center of the Roman practice of ancestor worship. The early Christians seem to have adapted this practice, shaping it into a belief in the soul and the worship of saints.

In general, the personal religious practices of the Romans abounded in myth, superstition, and magic. The public religion of the Romans consisted of an array of gods and goddesses, each representing an abstraction of some natural phenomena. The gods and goddesses were very anthropomorphic in nature and suffered most of the faults of ordinary men and women. These attributes of Roman religion were shared throughout the world of the Indo-Europeans.

The Romans, possibly from contact with the Hellenic Greeks or the Etruscans, developed a more spiritual attitude towards religion. The household gods, for example, became associated with abstract concepts of health, youth, memory, fortune, and many others. In this form they were not seen as being corporal in nature but rather as truly bodiless spirits. This spiritual aspect of being also applied to their belief in ghosts, demons, and other disembodied beings. This aspect of Roman belief also seems to have been carried into Christianity, particularly in the West. In general the Romans, as all ancient societies, seem to have been very flexible in their religious beliefs and adapted or adopted outright any religious belief that they came into contact with and thought useful.

The most striking aspect of early Roman religion was their organization of religion as part of the secular structure. The Romans, through their love of order and organization, created a religious structure that was taken over wholesale by early Christianity upon the fall of the empire. The leadership of the state religion was centered in a college of priests, with nine members. They were charged with the duties of keeping all historical annals, recording laws, and interpreting auguries. They also conducted all public sacrifices and ceremonies as well as conducting a periodic ritual purification of the city. They acted as the Supreme Court in the interpretation of the secular law. All aspects of the state religion were under the direct control of this college of priests. The king, as the head of the state religion, appointed the nine members of this college. Undoubtedly they were chosen from either the king's own family or the leading families of the tribes who elected the king. The duties of this college became more cumbersome, as the state grew larger, they created smaller colleges to which they delegated some to their duties. These colleges were placed in strategic locations throughout the area under Roman control.

The most important duty of the college appears to have been established in the college of augury. This college was assigned the duty of studying the intent of the gods by watching the flight of birds or by examining the entrails of sacrificed animals. At every important occasion or when major decisions had to be taken, whether religious or secular, the college of augury would be consulted. They would then read the signs and give a ruling as to the appropriateness of the contemplated action. This practice may have entered into Rome through the Etruscans or the Carthaginians who seem to have had similar practices. The concept of the infallible nature of the readings and pronouncements of the college of augury seems to have been adapted by the Christians into the concept of the infallibility of the pope. Due to the close attachment of the religious and secular aspects of Roman culture, the announcements made by these designated spokesmen seems to have been more formal than emotional. In general the public religion of the Romans seems to have been more a contract between the religious and secular aspects of society than a real emotional part of the day-to-day life of the Romans.

The secular side of the Roman culture was equally well organized. The hallmark of secular life was the concept of citizenship. Citizenship was originally based on membership in one of the original tribes. This citizenship was closely guarded by the various tribes and clans and soon became highly prized by all who obtained it. Citizenship carried with it certain duties as well as benefits. All citizens were subject to military service from their sixteenth birthday until their sixtieth birthday. During the republican period, only citizens could be a part of the military organization. A citizen was not allowed to enter into public service until he had served at least ten years in the military. As a result of the organization of citizens around the military, it soon became the most important part of most men's lives. The voting rights of the citizen were centered in the military and most of his rights as a citizen were based on military service.

During the republican period, the three original tribes were divided into thirty clans or curiae. The thirty curiae, through their leading families, were responsible for conferring on the elected officials the right to rule through the granting of the insignias of rule, i.e., the imperial eagles. A military assembly composed of "centuries" conducted the actual duties of the curiae through a delegation of power. This assembly chose the secular rulers, accepted or rejected the legislation presented by the senate, sat as the court of first instance on all secular cases of law, and decided the issue of war and peace in conjunction with the advice of the college of augury. This power, although it seems very broad, was limited by the power established in the representatives of the citizens at large. The whole body of the citizens elected the tribunes and consuls who were the only officials empowered to call the assembly. Once called, the assembly could only vote on the issues presented to them and they could not alter in any way the proposal that was submitted. This may have been the first example of a true separation of secular power between the different branches of government.

The senate was also originally elected by the vote of all the citizens and was charged with the duty of presenting the petitions of the people to the assembly for enactment. The senate was in actuality composed of the most illustrious of the leading families, as their wealth allowed them the time and education to serve. As the state grew in size and complexity, and the number of its citizens grew, the structure developed during the republican period became incompetent to conduct business in an orderly manner. The duties of electing the tribunes and consuls soon became a duty of appointment by the senate rather than election by the citizens. The senate also slowly absorbed the duties of the curiae. Through the consolidation of the powers of the curiae, military assembly, and tribunes the senate became the most powerful body in the state. As the body that now appointed the ruler of the secular state, who in turn elected the chief priests of the colleges, the senate soon controlled most aspects of Roman life. They were, however, unable to take direct control of the military, and the generals, who were in command of the troops.

As stated earlier, much of the religious and secular organization of the Roman culture was adopted wholesale by the later Christian Church. As the Romans moved to the east and established its control over an even larger area, two major weaknesses appeared in the republican system. The first was the lack of control over the military; and the second was the gathering of the power of the state into the hands of the wealthiest and most powerful families of the clans. These two factors quickly led to the demise of what little democracy had been allowed, and the republican institutions sank beneath the weight of the oligarchy created in the senate. This was the state of the republic by 100 BC. It was a state ruled by secular law and manned by citizens who had a great deal of loyalty to the state, both from their religious practice and from their participation in the secular government of the state.

The law also seems to have been something unique to the Roman society. Whether it was the law of tradition, i.e., the common law, or statutory law, it held a position in the minds of the Romans similar to that held by religion in the minds of other peoples. This law was already well organized and in most cases codified into a written system. The Roman system of law was adopted by the Christian Church as it took over the functions of the Roman state, and it was through the Church that the Roman law passed on to Western Europe. As with the peoples of Judaism, who had a comparable set of religious laws, the Romans placed a strong emphasis on education, and assured themselves of having a well-versed class of lawyers.

Essentially the Roman culture, as it existed under the republic, can be classified as a secular state controlled by secular law. The military, as well as the public service sector, was composed of citizens of the state. The citizens were very loyal to the state, due to the high value that was placed on being a citizen and the incorporation of the family structure as the sole support of citizenship. The typical Roman citizen was orderly, conservative, disciplined, and ultimately practical; indeed he was not much different from the later puritans that formed within later Christian Europe.

As the Romans continued their conquests into the east, they came into contact with well established peoples who found the Roman system alien to their beliefs. The Hellenic Greeks had been establishing themselves in the Near East for some two centuries, but during this time they had been unable to alter the cultures that were in place there prior to their conquest. They had been able to establish a thin veneer of Greek culture in the upper classes that occupied the major cities, and through this class of people had been able to affect the learning and material culture to a degree. The underlying population, however, was largely unaffected by the presence of the Hellenes. By the time that the Romans entered the picture, the older traditions of the Near East had again started to assert their dominance. Most importantly, the old established religions of the

Near East had again assumed the leading role in the lives of the people. Judaism had again been able to establish itself in Palestine, the Zoroastrian religion was again dominant in most of the Near East, and the Egyptians had again returned to the religion of the pharaohs. Only in Turkey and Greece proper was the old Greek culture to be found and then mostly in its Hellenistic form. We will come to a discussion of three of these movements, the consolidation of Judaism, the influence of the Persians, and the birth of Christianity. All three of these factors came to fruition during the long death throes of the Hellenic governance of the Near East.

The first in order of chronology is the Persian invasion of the Near East. The starting point of this invasion is unknown, but it is assumed that it began from the eastern shores of the Caspian Sea. The Medes, a related people, had migrated into northern Iran at an earlier date and had opened the doors for the later Persian migration. Initially the migration of the Medes and the Persians were stopped by the powerful state of Assyria. The Assyrians were a Semite people that had occupied the southern portions of Iran and Iraq for some centuries. For a short period the Medes and Persians were under the direct control of the Assyrians and they adopted the military know-how of the Assyrians. Around 500 BC, the Medes and Persians allied themselves with other Semitic tribes in southern Iraq and destroyed the Assyrian state. The Persians now quickly absorbed the peoples who occupied Iran, Iraq, Syria, Lebanon, Turkey, and Palestine. They even for a short time held sway over Egypt. They also moved into modern Afghanistan and took over the western end of the trade routes with the Far East. The Persians attempted to expand their empire into southern Russia, India, and Greece but were unable to establish any lasting control over these areas.

The Persians appear to have been very much like the Vedic peoples who had earlier moved into northwestern India. They were essentially a ruling military elite exercising control over a much larger underlying population of unrelated peoples. As a result, they were somewhat limited in the way that they affected these subject peoples. In Iran, they were able to become the dominant element in the population and therefore had their most extensive influence in this area. In the rest of the empire over a period of some 200 years, the Persians were slowly absorbed into the culture of the underlying peoples. They were content to allow the trade, the industries, the arts and crafts, and the literature to be conducted by the underlying populations. They established themselves as a military elite and maintained their status as a separate aristocratic class. Most of the trade, for example, remained in the hands of the Phoenician-, Greek- and Semitic-controlled caravans. They adapted the Assyrian system of writing to their own language but it seems to have been used mostly for the recording of official occurrences. They exerted the most influence in three areas; the secular government, the military, and the state religion.

Early in the history of the Persians, probably while they were still in their original homeland, a prophet arose among them named Zarathustra. Zarathustra, whose Greek name was Zoroaster, believed in and advocated a supreme god of light known as Ahura-Mazda. Ahura-Mazda appeared to Zarathustra and revealed to him the ideas that later became the book of revelations known as the Avesta. This was commonly translated as the book of knowledge and wisdom. Ahura-Mazda told him to go forth and preach the word of god as revealed in the Avesta. At first, Zarathustra was ridiculed by the people, but eventually the religion was accepted by the high prince of Iran (Vishtaspa), who agreed to spread the religion throughout the empire. Such was the birth of the Zoroastrian religion.

When Zarathustra found the Medes and Persians, they were worshipping animals, ancestors, the sun and earth, in a religion that had much in common with all other Indo-European peoples. The chief god at this time was the sun god, Mithra. Others included Anaita, the goddess of fertility, and Haoma, the bull god. Haoma was seen as a god that had died and rose again and offered mankind his blood as the means of obtaining immortality.

Zarathustra attacked both this religion and its priesthood, who were known as the magi, with all the zeal that prophets are known for. Upon his ascension to power, the Persian ruler Darius I accepted the religion of Zarathustra and made it the official state religion. The Avesta was accepted as the bible of the Zoroastrians; it consisted of the collected sayings and prayers of the prophet. Within the Avesta one finds the contributions of earlier religions, especially the Vedic book known as the Rig Veda, which was incorporated nearly word for word in some passages. There are also several passages that represent a direct borrowing of earlier Babylonian myth, such as the world being created in six periods (days), the descent of all of humanity from one set of parents, the establishment of an earthly paradise, the discontent of the creator with his creation and its destruction in a general flood.

There are, however, as many elements that are Persian, and there are elements of a foreign nature. The Persians began by combining the two major deities Ahura and Mithra into a dual god known as Ahura-Mazda. The tenets of the new religion included the belief, that the world is conceived as a dualism not found in other earlier religions. This dualism is seen as the battle between good (Ahura-Mazda) and the evil (Ahriman), a conflict which would last for 12,000 years. Purity and honesty are seen as the greatest virtues for the Zoroastrian and in themselves will lead to an everlasting life. The dead must not be buried, as with the Greeks and Semites, or burned, as with the Indians, but left exposed to be consumed by birds and other animals that eat carrion. Ahura-Mazda was not seen as having a corporeal body but rather as a spiritual substance that encompassed the whole of the universe.

For the Zoroastrian, the material and the spiritual were one and that one was Ahura-Mazda. Ahura-Mazda as creator and ruler of the universe was supported by a legion of lesser beings that were corporeal and were seen as abstractions of natural phenomena, such as fire, water, sun, moon, and many others. Ahura-Mazda was seen as supreme, as the "good mind," a concept that was essentially the same as the Greek concept of the logos.

This attempt at establishing a type of monotheism was quickly converted to polytheism by the followers of the religion. The abstract lesser beings became known as Amesha Spenda or the immortal ones. In addition to these holy spirits, there were also guardian angels for each man, woman and child. The holy spirits and the angels helped mankind to stay on the path of righteousness. As a counter-balance there were also seven daevas, or evil spirits, that continually tempted man away from the path of righteousness. Their leader was, of course, Ahriman. Ahriman, in the Avesta, was portrayed much in the same manner as Satan in the Old Testament. It was Ahriman who had destroyed the original paradise that had been created for man. Zarathustra, himself, seems to have disregarded the evil spirits, seeing them as mere abstractions of natural processes that hinder the progress of mankind.

The Zoroastrian religion slowly lost its place in the state to the underlying religion of Mithra. Ahura-Mazda was absorbed into the figure of Mithra and the magi established themselves as the official priesthood. The magi adopted a form of asceticism so austere that they even earned the admiration of the Greeks for their great wisdom. This asceticism also included a strict monogamy that was unusual for the time. The practices of the magi again show a close similarity to the practices established within the Hindu faith. In both cases, the early logic of the Indo-Europeans was replaced by a reliance on poetry and myth.

The ethic of the Zoroastrians was based on the Golden Rule. The duty of man was seen as three-fold: to love your enemy, to turn the wicked to the paths of righteousness, and to teach the ignorant. The greatest virtue was piety, followed closely by honor and honestly in action and speech. This ethic of generosity and kindliness did not extend to those who were outside the faith, and others were treated much the same as they were in other religions.

Zoroastrians saw foreigners as inferior beings that had been tricked by Ahura-Mazda into loving their own country to keep them from attacking Persia. The Zoroastrians did not use temples or idols, but established simple altars on hill-tops, in the palaces, and at the center of the city. They also considered the family hearth to be a sacred altar. As with the Romans, the fires, both in the hearth and in the public altars, were to be kept burning continuously. The sacrifices of the Zoroastrian were not different in kind from those of other religions, but only the odor was received by the god and the material substance was to be eaten and drunk by the priests and the people. The magi explained that the gods only wanted the soul of the sacrificial victim. The souls of the dead were believed to pass over a sifting bridge: The good would be allowed to pass over the bridge and enter paradise, while the wicked would be thrown from the bridge into hell. Hell consisted of seven different levels and the wicked would enter whichever level matched the level of his or her wickedness. At the end of the 12,000-year cycle, Ahura-Mazda would bring the world to a last judgment, at which time Ahriman would be destroyed. Just as in India, the 12,000 years was seen as a continuing cycle, with the world passing over and over again through the same process of creation and destruction.

The secular government of the Persians consisted of dividing the empire into satrapies, or provinces, which to a large degree matched the boundaries of established custom and language. At its height the empire consisted of twenty such provinces: Egypt, Palestine, Syria, Phoenicia (Lebanon), Lydia, Phrygia, Ionia (northwestern Turkey), Cappadocia, Cilicia, Armenia (central and southern Turkey), Assyria (northern Iraq), the Caucasus (northern Turkey), Babylonia (southern Iraq), Medea, Persia (Iran) Afghanistan, Baluchistan (Turkmenistan and Uzbekistan), India west of the Indus (Pakistan) Sogdiana, Bactria, and the territory of the Massageta (the Crimea, around the Black Sea). The basis of Persian rule was the military, which consisted initially of only Medes and Persians. Each male was to be available for military service from his fifteenth to his fiftieth birthday. The main army was stationed at or near the capital in Iran, with large contingents stationed in each of the satrapies. In addition, each of the satrapies had to furnish a contingent of its own native soldiers, who were kept separate from the state military and maintained their own language, weapons, and method of fighting. The king was the sole law-giver and his word was seen as divine, leading to the Persian belief that their law never changed. The king was also the Supreme Court, but this function was delegated to a learned elder who was supported by a high court of justice. Local courts were spread throughout the empire and took their lead from the high court. The satrapies were ruled in the name of the king, but were actually ruled by persons appointed by the king or in some cases by the native ruling class. The king, as a means of controlling the satraps, instituted a system of internal police and left the control of the military in the hands of only Medes and Persians. Underneath this structure was a vast native bureaucracy that was inherited by the Persians and maintained its own customs and language. In support of this system, the Persian government built a series of good roads that allowed ease of access throughout the empire. The Romans later adopted this system of road building. The bureaucracy could, and did, endure and outlast all changes that took place at the top. Each religion that was found in the empire was allowed to maintain its unique brand of worship, laws, customs, morals, and commercial activities.

The Persians were able to maintain their empire for some two hundred years. During this period, the Persian aristocracy had given itself up to luxury and had expended their energy in war, allowing the twenty satrapies to essentially become twenty independent nations. The vacuum created by the degeneration of the ruling aristocracy was filled by the invading Macedonians. The Macedonians, who were essentially Greek in culture, adapted wholesale the traditions of the Persians in respect to their method of ruling the empire. They established themselves as a military elite and were able to influence the underlying peoples in the same degree as the former Persian rulers. They continued the Persian toleration of religion, the Persian use of the native peoples as a working bureaucracy and the use of the native peoples in conduct of the trading, industrial, and intellectual activities. In total, the Persian and Macedonian ascendancy can be seen as a period of 400 years of relative peace for the underlying populations (always subject, of course, to the incursions of the wars of the military elite).

During this period a separate and distinct evolution was occurring in Palestine, which involved the final consolidation of Judaism. The early history of Judaism revolves around two separate periods of captivity. The first occurred about 1800 BC and entailed the removal of some, or all, of the Hebrews from their homeland in Arabia to Egypt. At this time, the Hebrews seem to have been a rather loose confederation of twelve tribes. It is unknown whether all the tribes were taken captive or just some part of them. Some tribes, according to the Biblical account, seem to have followed the captured tribes into Egypt voluntarily. The Biblical tradition indicates that the Hebrews remained in Egypt for some four centuries. The conditions under which the Hebrews lived in Egypt are not currently known, but it can be assumed that they maintained a separate existence from the Egyptians. It appears that the Egyptians had some system by which captured peoples were established as enclaves within the general population and allowed to maintain their language and customs. Whatever the method, the Hebrews seem to have maintained their national identity and language for a period of some 400 years.

At the end of this captivity, the religion the Hebrews had brought with them began to take on the tenets of later Judaism. The Biblical account, as well as the traditional mythology of the Hebrews, asserts that the god of Israel (that is, of the people of Israel) heard their prayers to be released from captivity and appeared to Moses, promising him deliverance. God explained to Moses that he had chosen the people of Israel to be his priesthood on earth. God also promised Moses that he would lead them out of Egypt and establish them in a Promised

Land. This was the covenant established between God and the Hebrews. The Biblical account records the miracles that god allowed Moses to perform to force the Pharaoh to release the Hebrews. It also details the actual exodus from Egypt including the destruction of the pharaoh and his forces in the Red Sea. The Hebrews were then subjected to a period of forty years of wandering in the desert before reaching the Promised Land. During this journey, God again appeared to Moses and delivered his laws for the people in their worship of him. This revelation included the Ten Commandments, which were originally believed to have been written in stone, and the revelations given orally to Moses by God that later became known as the Torah (oral law) of Judaism. The oral tradition (Torah) that developed at this time was later incorporated into a written version which is essentially the first five books of the Old Testament. The first period of captivity, therefore, established the three basic components of Judaism: the fact that the people of Israel were the chosen people of god, that they had received a divine promise to be established in the holy land, and that their laws were the result of the direct revelation of god to man.

During the next seven centuries (from approximately 1,400 BC until 700 BC), the people of Israel were fully engaged in efforts to win the Holy Land (Palestine) from the control of the Canaanites and others who occupied it. During most of this period, the Hebrews were only one of many tribes that occupied the area; the portion that was under their control, they called the land of Judah. This was the period during which such men as David and Solomon ruled over the people of Israel. During this period there was also a high level of activity by prophets, such as Isaiah and Joshua. These prophecies were later incorporated into the Hebrew tradition, but at this time the religion of Judaism seems to have been largely a matter of oral tradition. Although there were undoubtedly many developments within the traditions of Judaism during this period, the mainstay of the religion seems to have been the three basic tenets established at the exodus (departure from Egypt). The main line of development seems to have been in the form of the oral traditions surrounding the exodus, the prophets, and the development of the law. The latter consisted of the religious practices, such as circumcision, the prohibition against eating pork or blood, and rituals of sacrifice. During this period, Judaism was established as the first and probably only existing religion that held faithfully to the concept of monotheism. Near the end of this period the Hebrews had been able to establish themselves in Palestine and had adopted an urban culture. They built their first temple as a symbol of their religion, which housed the Ark of the Covenant and contained the holy of holies. This was the only visible sign of their worship, as they rejected all use of altars and idols. The temple itself was less a place of worship than a place where the people could meet and be instructed in the law of the faith. The concept of the temple was the model used in the establishment of the synagogue after the Hebrews were ejected from the Holy Land for the last time in 70 BC by the Romans. This first temple was destroyed at the time that the Hebrews were carried into their second period of captivity.

About 600 BC, the Hebrew lands were invaded by the Assyrians and the Hebrews were again carried away as captives, this time to the city of Babylon. This captivity lasted only some fifty years, but represents a great turning point in the religion of Judaism. From the Biblical and traditional accounts, this captivity threatened to fundamentally undermine the religion of Judaism. The people were quickly falling into the ways of the Babylonians and forgetting their Hebrew heritage. In an effort to halt this movement, the leaders of the Hebrews wrote down the oral traditions. The first five books of the Old Testament seem to have been the result of this process. In writing down the oral traditions, they also seem to have included many of the beliefs that they encountered in Babylon. Some of these included the creation story which is now found in Genesis, the story of the Garden of Eden and the fall of the first man, the concept of heaven and hell, and the story of the great flood. It also appears that Judaism adopted its concern with the last judgment and redemption of the people from Babylonian traditions.

These alien traditions were skillfully woven into the earlier oral traditions of the Hebrews and became part of what they presented as the revealed word of god. They lent a long term support to the three basic tenets of Judaism, that is, that the people were chosen by god, that they had inherited the Holy Land from god, and that their laws and traditions were handed down directly from god. As a part of the effort to slow down the incorporation of their people into the culture of Babylon, the leaders also instituted a fierce commitment to study, among the people (particularly study of their holy scriptures, but also a general respect for learning). The severity of their beliefs, coupled with the practice of circumcision, seems to have been the major reason for the limited appeal of Judaism to the other people with whom Judaism came into contact.

This period of captivity ended with the Persian invasion under Cyrus, around 600 BC. Cyrus restored the Hebrews to Judah (Palestine) and rebuilt their temple. During the 200 year rule of the Persians, and the 200 year rule of the Hellenes that followed, the Hebrews were able to occupy Palestine in relative peace. Most experts think that it was during this period of peace and independence that the remainder of the Old Testament was written down. In doing so, the Hebrews incorporated some of the traditions that had come to them through the Persians. They apparently accepted as part of their belief the Persian concept of dualism (good vs. evil), the personal responsibility of the individual for righteous behavior, and others. It is also during this period, experts believe, that the tradition began of writing commentaries on the Jewish civil and religious law. These traditions, in written form, seem to have obtained to their modern form by roughly 100 BC. With the invasion of the Romans, the independent history of the Jewish state comes to an end (until Israel was reestablished in 1948). The Romans again destroyed the temple. The state of

Judea was incorporated into the larger province of Syria. Judaism as a religion continued to exist without any attachment to a secular state.

At this time, Judaism seems to have split up into several different sects. The two largest and most important were the Pharisees and the Sadducees. A smaller but important sect was called by the name Essene; this sect seems to have had an important impact on early Christianity, although the details have yet to be confirmed. The Essenes are thought to have established themselves as a group of ascetics living in the caves around Jerusalem. They were extremely strict in the observance of the laws of Judaism and had removed themselves from normal society to prevent their pollution by looser ways of life. They considered the practices of both the Pharisees and the Sadducees as deviating from the laws as established by the Old Testament and the Talmud. However, it appears that both of these sects were relatively pure in their practice of Judaism; the Sadducees tended to be a little more conservative and puritanical. The main difference between them lies in the attempt by the Pharisees to incorporate the thought and beliefs of Greek mysticism into the Hebrew tradition. Judaism, however, seems to have been much more resistant to the influence of Greek thought than the later religions of Christianity and Islam. It appears that the teaching of the Essene sect, concerning its rejection of the practices of the other two sects, brought about the attempt by Christ to reform Judaism.

After the Roman conquest, and its opening of the entire empire to all peoples, the Jewish people began what later became known as the Diaspora or dispersion. Having found themselves homeless they, mainly through their trading activities, began to establish communities throughout the empire. As this process continued, the Jewish population that remained in Jerusalem became less capable of controlling Judaism. Although the Jews do not seem to have been forced to live in segregated communities, the establishment of the Synagogue seems to have encouraged a voluntary segregation. The fact of the Synagogue being the center of teaching and instruction for the adherents of

Judaism also tended to create living quarters that were densely crowded around the Synagogue, as adherents needed to stay close to the center of religious life and instruction. The dispersion, coupled with the synagogue tradition, also helped to consolidate the tenets of Judaism into a relatively unchanging set of traditions. Judaism remained insulated from outside influences for many centuries. It remains to be seen whether or not the taking on of secular responsibilities will alter the way in which Judaism is practiced.

The third major development occurred just before the Roman takeover of Palestine. It was an integral part of the slow decay of authority within the Persian and Macedonian over-lordships. This third movement is the birth of Christianity, within the confines of Judaism.

Even though it occurred during a time in which one could expect an extensive written record, that is not the case. Jesus did not write down any of his teachings, and the apostles and others did not begin to do so for some sixty years after the death of Christ. The Christian sect itself, like Judaism, was not significant enough to require comment by the Persians, Hellenes, or Romans. The earliest mention of Christians in the Roman records appears sixty years after Christ. Even the extant records of Judaism from that period do not mention the teachings of Christ. This has led many people to contemplate the possibility that Christ was a myth, along the order of Buddha and other great religious leaders whose actual existence is doubtful. Whether or not Christ was a historical person or merely a "virtual" figure that represents a certain collection of thoughts and teachings does not matter for our purposes. It is the basic foundations of the Christian religion that are being sought, regardless of their source. For our purposes, we can accept that Christ was a historical person and that the gospels as written by Mark, Matthew and Luke are accurate transmissions of his teachings.

It is generally accepted that the teachings of Christ began as attempts to reform Judaism and bring its adherents back to a more strict observance of the law. The Pharisees in particular were the target of Christ's reform efforts. As we have seen, they tended to accommodate the Greek learning to the traditions of Judaism, which the more conservative sects interpreted as a form of skepticism. In fact, the Pharisees did tend to relax some of the more severe traditions, such as the requirement that Jewish people not charge interest on loans. Initially, Christ claimed only that he came to teach the law as it existed in Judaism, not to overthrow that law. He does not seem to have claimed any sort of divinity within himself, initially, but possibly held himself out as a prophet. He did not claim that he had any spiritual relation to the people who lived outside the faith of Judaism.

The earliest of the gospels appeared about sixty years after the death of Christ and is believed to be that of Matthew. This may in fact be the only gospel that was written by a person who actually knew Christ while he was alive. The gospels of Mark and Luke are generally believed to have been written by men who studied under former disciples of Christ. The only gospel that was obviously written long after the death of Christ was the gospel of John. By the end of the first century after Christ, there were literally hundreds of testaments of his teachings. These testaments were generally known as the Acts. The four gospels that make up the modern New Testament, along with the book of Acts (which is also believed to have been written by Luke), eventually were accepted as the most faithful accounts. The acceptance of these writings had definitely been accomplished by AD 300.

During the first two centuries after the death of Christ, the followers of Christ established communities throughout the Roman Empire. The communities were normally established within the already existing Jewish communities and represented the attempted conversion of the Jewish communities to Christianity. At first, the Romans were unable to make any distinction between the Christian and Jewish members of their population.

Two of the major figures that were involved with the establishment of Christian communities were Peter and Paul. Neither of them had known Christ or any of his disciples. Peter was most active in establishing Christian communities in Palestine, Arabia, and Egypt but is also credited with establishing the Christian community in Rome. Paul, who was a Roman citizen and had received a classical education, was active in Asia Minor, Syria, Macedonia and Cyprus. Paul apparently was at odds with Peter and the community of Palestine as to the tenets of Christian belief. The early Christian communities established by the disciples of Christ, or those appointed by them, tended to remain Jewish in ritual and spirit, but somewhat more puritanical in their practice than the rest of the Jewish community. Paul was much more lenient in his attitude towards ritual. He had been trained in the classical lore of his time, specifically neo-Platonism and neo-Pythagoreanism, both of which have played a large part in the Catholic and Orthodox versions of Christianity (the tenets of this schools include the concepts of the logos, or word, the in corporeality of the spiritual world and many others). He also seems to have become acquainted with the Hindu tradition of asceticism. Early in the history of Christianity, the various communities had broken up into a large number of sects each with its own set of beliefs and practices. This was countered to some degree by the communities that were located in the large cities of the empire, especially those located in Jerusalem, Antioch, Alexandria, Carthage, and Rome.

Paul's teaching was tempered by his classical education and his teaching was much more mystical than what was taught by the other communities who had adapted the practical approach of Judaism. All of the communities, however, had a basic set of beliefs that they held in common: the belief in God and that God had sent his son to earth to redeem the sins of mankind with his death on the cross, and that the Bible represented the actual word of god in a literal sense. In addition to these basic beliefs, which may be the only ones that were taught by Christ or his disciples, they also accepted many of the doctrines of Judaism, such as the concept of heaven and hell, the concept of the last judgment, and the establishment of the kingdom of god on earth. They did reject the practice of circumcision (as inhibiting the conversion of gentiles), and many of the taboos of Judaism.

As time passed, the community in Rome — benefiting from the fact that it was the capital of the empire — gained precedence over those in other cities. The Christian community located in Rome, early in the growth of Christianity, then became the center of decision on disputes concerning theology and ritual. The Roman community had already borrowed much organizational skill from the Romans and could hold itself out with some authority. The Christians of Jerusalem had slowly reverted to Judaism, which reduced this city in importance within the faith — at least, in matters of theology and ritual. Egypt and North Africa had adopted the Hindu tradition of asceticism and at this time also were not as important in these matters as they later became. The leading cities in the Christian movement at the early stages were those located in modern Turkey and Macedonia, and Rome, all of whom were greatly influence by the teachings of Paul.

By the time of the fall of the Western Roman Empire around AD 500, most of the basic tenets of Christianity had been established firmly into Christian theology. As we shall see, there were many controversies still to be settled but the outline was clear. The basics had been established, the empire had accepted Christianity as the official state religion under the teaching of Paul, Rome had established itself as the leader in theological and ritual disputes, and Rome had already adopted wholesale the organizational skill of the Romans along with a large share of their secular traditions. Both the later Roman Catholic Church and the Greek Orthodox Church had accepted as authoritative the teachings of Paul and had already brought most of the other communities into the Pauline tradition.

The early development of Christianity can be clearly designated as a reform movement aimed at the reestablishment of strict discipline within Judaism. Over a period of some 300 years, the Christian religion broke into a large number of sects as it disassociated itself from Judaism. They all maintained a basic set of beliefs, but each also had its own interpretation of the scriptures, allowing for a considerable variation in actual practice. By the end of the 300 years of initial growth the Christian faith had coalesced into three major factions, specifically, the Roman Catholic Church, the Greek Orthodox Church, and the Monastic movement that was essentially limited to Africa. The basic beliefs that united all three of these sects were the belief that both the Old and New Testaments were the literal word of God, that Christ was God incarnate on earth, and that Christ had come to redeem the sins of mankind through his death on the cross. The differences that separated these sects tended to be more involved with the fine points of theology and ritual rather than basic questions of faith.

The period of Roman dominance in most of Europe, northern Africa, and the Near East, until about AD 476, can be seen as the slow shift from the classical world to the beginnings of the modern world. The written religions, or religions that depended on a divinely inspired book, began to replace totally the older traditions of the Near East and Egypt. They also replaced the Greek and Roman traditions to a large degree with the arrival of the new peoples who overthrew the Western Roman Empire. In doing so, they incorporated into their theological systems all that they thought was valuable in the older traditions. The result was the consolidation of Judaism into the form that it has maintained from the dispersal from Palestine until the present day. It was also the period during which Christianity broke from its parent religion, Judaism, and began to evolve into a religion of its own.

The Romans, as a people and as an organized state, were completely destroyed or absorbed by the peoples who overran them at the end of the 5th century AD. The only survival of the Roman Empire in the west was the Roman

Catholic Church and the traditions of the remaining Roman aristocracy that survived for a time in Spain, France, and especially Italy. In the east, a slow conversion of the Romans had been taking place as they continued to be absorbed into the Greek traditions of the Hellenes. In Europe, the traditions of the Greeks (Hellenes), and to a large extent the heritage of the Romans, were lost to the memory of mankind — hence the term "Dark Ages." In the east, the Byzantine Empire, which replaced the Roman Empire in those regions, was largely Greek in culture and used the Greek language. This accentuated the differences between the Catholic and Orthodox churches. Byzantium was essentially an isolated empire that existed in a sea of less civilized peoples. In essence, the classical world of the Persians, Greeks, Macedonians, and Romans had come to an end.

In relationship to the debate between atheism and religion, the following points should be made. First, in Europe, with both the western and eastern portions of the old Roman Empire, religion had won a complete victory over the skepticism brought forth by the classical tradition. This tradition of skeptical thought with its emphasis on human reason would be lost to Europe for many centuries. In the Near East, a somewhat different picture can be drawn. The Judaic love of learning and teaching would incorporate the Greek/Hellenic traditions within their system of learning in a somewhat altered form. We will see the effect that this incorporation had on the reawaking of Europe, in a later chapter. Here, it is enough to state that Arab and Jewish scholars in northern Africa and Moorish Spain, as well as, the Near East, kept alive the traditions lost to Europe through the centuries of what is called the dark ages. The ancient Persian traditions were also kept alive by the peoples who occupied Iran and most of Iraq. These peoples also maintained a strong contact with the traditions of the even older Babylonian cultures. Outside of Judaism and the new religion of Christianity, the older religious traditions of the Near East had also reached the end of their vital growth and existence. They continue to exist, in some cases, to this day, but have generally been absorbed into the traditions of Islam that will be dealt with later.

It is worth noting in passing that the two great eastern cultures, i.e., India and China, would remain within their classical traditions for many centuries to come. The great Hindu tradition had given birth to several new religions, including Buddhism, but had reverted to the Hindu tradition. Buddhism was to become the dominant religion of Southeast Asia long before the birth of Christianity and it would remain the main tradition of the area until this very day. Buddhism also entered and made an impact on Tibet, China, Korea, Japan and Mongolia but has been somewhat overtaken in China by Confucianism and later by Communism. Buddhism and related religions have also to a large degree been replaced by Islam in Central Asia and northwestern China; and by Christianity in Korea. China, of course, is officially a country that is atheistic, but in practical terms is probably as religious as it was prior to communism. These areas are outside the scope of this book but a full analysis of religion would require their study in another place.

From the position of atheism, it is important to understand that most the basic beliefs of the religions discussed above are now deeply buried within the traditions of the new religions. That the traditions of the older religions were adopted and adapted to new conditions cannot be questioned. They do not, however, truly represent a living tradition any longer and it will now be necessary to follow the development of the new religions (Christianity, Judaism, and Islam) to their current state of beliefs. It will also be necessary, towards the end of this period, to follow the reawakening of skepticism and its evolution into atheism.

CHAPTER 4. CHRISTIANITY, PERSIA AND ISLAM

The period from the fall of the Western Roman Empire until the rise of the modern nation states is one of the busiest in all history, at least in relation to Europe and our American heritage. It covers the period running from roughly AD 600 to 1300. Four trends that occurred during this period deserve to be highlighted, as they affected every aspect of European religious experience and illustrate that religious beliefs and tenets of have shifted through the centuries; they are neither "cast in stone" nor transmitted in an immutable form by some supernatural entity.

The first of the four trends is the continued development of the Christian religion through its major arms — the Roman Catholic Church, the Greek Orthodox Church, and the monastic movement. The second is the growth of atheism within the confines of Christian Europe. The third is the birth and growth of Islam in the Near East and its rapid spread to both Africa and Asia. The fourth is the continued development of Judaism, and its effect on Islam, and the establishment and growth of the Sassanid dynasty in Persia and its effects on

Islam. In combination, these trends set the stage upon which the modern world would act out its drama and still does.

The forces of Alexander the Great defeated the original Persians in 333 BC, and replaced their dynasty with that of the Parthians, who were also known as the Arsacid dynasty. Later the Sassanids, direct ancestors of the original Persians, took over the empire of the Parthians, and for a period of some 400 years controlled the area stretching from the eastern shores of the Black Sea to the western shores of the Caspian Sea, southward through Iran and Iraq and eastward into what are modern Afghanistan, Pakistan, and Turkmenistan. During this 400-year period they also held short periods of rule over Arabia, Syria, Palestine and Egypt. They even made several incursions into what we know as Turkey. They were, however, constantly at war with the less civilized tribes that occupied southern Russia and the rest of Central Asia and could not direct their attention to the west consistently; however, they did maintain a constant border battle with the Byzantine Empire (Eastern Roman Empire) around the shores of the Black Sea. Not much remains to assist the research of modern historians concerning their art, written records or their actual day-to-day lives. From the records that do remain and from the records of the Byzantines and Islamic peoples, the following outline can be drawn.

The Sassanids restored the Zoroastrian religion as the official state religion of their empire. They also restored the Persian tradition of a high level of tolerance for other religions that were found in the empire. The Sassanids, like the followers of Judaism and later Islam, do not seem to have made any separation of the secular and religious life. The priests (magi) were normally in charge of administering and adjudicating the laws, which they also helped to legislate. The king as the divine representative was the main law-giver and, as with the older Persian tradition, his laws were divine and not subject to change. The aristocratic class (or military elite) conducted the actual day-to-day operation of the government, with support provided by the priests. The administration of the empire seems to have been very efficient and was supported by a good system of roads, well-provisioned naval ports, post offices, and other innovations.

About AD 600, when the Sassanids were brought to an end by the invasion of Islamic forces, they had already reached a point of exhaustion and did not put up a fight. Islam was to adopt wholesale the systems initiated by the Sassanids. Many of the later refinements of Islamic culture were directly inherited from the Persians. One major factor that shaped Islam was the college that had been established at Jundi-I-Shapur for the education of the royal Persian family, as well as the children of the leading aristocratic families. During the 5th century of our era, this college was considered to be the intellectual capital of the known world.

The importance of the Sassanids is twofold. They appear to have been the major influence on the growth and development of Islam after its initial foundation, and they seem to have been the main bulwark stopping the advance of less civilized peoples out of southern Russia and Central Asia. The challenges of fending off the eastern hordes brought them to military and financial bankruptcy after 400 years of almost constant warfare.

During the same period, the religion of Judaism was attempting to come to terms with the dispersion of its adherents. The Jewish people had launched several revolts against those who controlled the area of Palestine, but they had all been savagely defeated and the Jewish population of Palestine, depleted by these battles, was largely replaced with Arabic peoples. By the time Islam was emerging, the Jewish community in Palestine had lost its leadership of Judaism, as evidenced by its loss of the right to set the calendar for Jewish holidays and the adjudication of Jewish law. There were many Jewish communities outside of Palestine, and the most significant were those located in southern Iraq, Arabia, North Africa, Sicily, Cyprus, Spain and France. There were also large communities in Turkey and Constantinople, but these were much more strictly controlled by the Byzantine rulers.

As the process of dispersion continued, it became much more difficult for the oral traditions of the Jewish law to be memorized and passed down from generation to generation. Up to that point, the written record of Judaism had been limited to the Old Testament and some portions of the law. The Old Testament had always been supported by the oral law, which was also believed to have been given by God to Moses on Mt. Sinai. From that time onward, it is supposed to have been memorized by certain members of the faith and passed down to new generations.

By about AD 100, the oral law had begun to diversify; different regions had different understandings of the law. In order to limit and control its evolution, the leaders committed it to writing; this became known as the Mishnah. The Mishnah is the authoritative source of the religious law of Judaism. After another five or six centuries of discussion, commentary and interpretation of the Mishnah by the learned leaders of Judaism, two sets of written commentary (the Gemara) were composed by the schools located in Palestine and Babylon (the Babylonian Gemara is four times longer than the Palestinian one). The Talmud is the combination of the Mishnah and the two Gemaras.

By the time Islam arrived, the tenets of Judaism had been converted into three distinct types of written records: the Old Testament, which had existed in written form for some time, the Mishnah, and the two Gemaras. One of the main differences between the Sadducees and the Pharisees concerned the issue of whether or not the oral laws were divinely inspired. The Sadducees held the position that the oral law was not divinely inspired and therefore was not a binding force. The Pharisees believed that it was. The Sadducees ceased to be a factor when Judah fell to the Romans, leaving the tradition supported by the Pharisees in control. Both the communities at Palestine and Babylon accepted that position.

Since the Jewish people were not living in one distinct area but had settled in different centers throughout Europe, the Mediterranean and the Middle East, they do not have a secular history per se. The religion of Judaism is a day-to-day confrontation with God. Judaism is a religion pure and simple and controls every aspect of the lives of its adherents, with the possible exception their participation in the societies to which they belong.

The theology contained in the Talmud is above all a code of ethics. It differs greatly from that of Christianity but is very like that of Islam. The tenets of Judaism show clearly the belief that moral behavior cannot be left for support solely on human reason. Only the fear of God coupled with eternal rewards and punishments is enough to curb the natural desires of mankind. The moral code is based upon the fact that God sees and records all that is done by the individual. The balance between evil and good in the individual is established at the day of the last judgment, when eternal rewards and punishments are handed out. As stated earlier, secular law and social ethics were not considered as separate from the religion of Judaism. There was no distinction between crime and sin, secular law and religious law, or public and private behavior. The basic rules of individual morality revolved around the sanctity of the family, the honor due the parents of each individual as well as to the elderly in general, and a charitable disposition to all. As a result, celibacy and childlessness were seen as major sins. Because the law allowed polygamy, adultery was treated as a capital crime. The Talmud takes great care in fostering the control of the senses; the body and the soul are strictly separated. The body is of this earth and passes away at death, while the soul is of God and is subject to the last judgment. One of the highest duties in Judaism is the loving care of children coupled with their education in the law. Divorce, by law, was allowed upon mutual consent, but in practice it was made difficult by obstacles both social and financial in nature. The law was clearly male-orientated — to such a degree that the power of women seems to have been truly feared by the religious leaders.

95

The Talmud also contains much teaching concerning rituals, especially cleanliness, taboos, magic, incantations, history, medicine, and other topics. Essentially, the Talmud incorporated into itself the literature that normally would have been part of the secular literature of a people who represent a nation. It was intended to, and did, affect every aspect of the individual's life and through the use of a common ritual tended to unify the Jewish people, no matter where they were found. The fact that they have survived centuries of dispersal without the unifying factor of a national homeland testifies to the success of the Talmud in helping to forge a unified people. The severity and complexity of the law included within the Talmud seems to account for the exclusiveness of the Jewish peoples and the lack of interest on the part of others who might normally be expected to merge with them. It may also explain why both Christianity and Islam were initially seen as movements that were attempts to bring Judaism a wider interest to non-Judaic peoples, rather than as independent religious developments.

In their secular life the adherents of Judaism, for the most part not forced to do so, voluntarily lived in segregated communities. The synagogue was the center of Jewish life and the Jewish communities formed around the synagogue as closely as possible. Overcrowding resulted, creating slums and engendering a large degree of suspicion in the surrounding population. In rural areas as well, the Jews stayed apart from others and, abiding by their centuries-old rituals, they came to follow different practices and hold to different standards than their neighbors. The Jewish peoples, as a result, often came to be restricted by the surrounding population, including in terms of commercial and financial activities.

By the time of the advent of Islam, Judaism had arrived at its current system of theology and ritual. For the next 1,200 years, the Jewish populations would maintain their tight exclusiveness and separation from other peoples.

Taxation and confiscation of Jewish property soon drove the Jewish people out of agriculture and into urban pursuits. Once established in the urban society, they became very adept at various crafts, over which they established a virtual monopoly, until legal restrictions again intervened. They then developed a successful position in international trade, and came to dominate that field. The wealth that this trade brought them again put them in the public eye and raised suspicions; measures were again taken to curb their success. They then moved into the financial arena, backing many of the new industrial enterprises and governments of Europe. They soon became the leading source of loans, especially in the newly forming nation states of Europe. Once again, however, the taxation and confiscation of Jewish wealth by the Christians and Moslems became an unbearable burden for the Jewish communities. In the regions where there was less persecution (as in most of the Moslem countries), the Jewish people were able to display a talent in the secular fields of law and administration seldom matched by other peoples. The emotional and intellectual strength and the unity of the Jewish people as a whole allowed them to maintain a behind-the-scenes importance that cannot be denied. They continue to this day to represent one of the most powerful influences in every society in which they participate.

Christianity also underwent a large-scale evolution as the centuries passed. Perhaps the greatest changes had to do with the political factors involved — the establishment of the Byzantine Empire (which was largely Greek in culture), and the disintegration of the Western Roman Empire. The Byzantine Empire, early in its history, subjected the Christian Church to its authority, reducing its flexibility in dealing with the changes that occurred in the empire. In the west, the Roman Catholic Church to a very large degree inherited the functions of the defunct secular Roman government. Within these two major developments, the monastic movement spread throughout all Europe from its base in Africa and Syria.

Three major events stand out in the evolution of the Roman Catholic Church within the Western Empire. The first was the conversion of Emperor Constantine to Christianity, which took place towards the end of the dominance of the secular Roman government. Constantine established Christianity as the official state religion, releasing Christians from all persecution. As a result, Christianity was forced to take on new responsibilities as the official religion. The church quickly adopted the administrative, legal, and economic genius of the secular Romans to its own internal organization. By the time that the empire began to be overrun by barbarians, the Roman Catholic Church had remade itself into a well-organized administrative unit and had exerted its influence on all the Christian communities then in existence. It had also established itself as an independent political and economic power within the empire, by gathering together church-owned estates.

The second factor in the evolution of the Roman Church came about through the acceptance of the teachings of Augustine. Augustine spent most of his life as the Bishop of Hippo in North Africa. His first task as Bishop was to defeat the heresy known as Donatism: the Donatists denied the efficacy of the sacraments administered by priests in a state of sin. The Roman Church rejected this position as harmful to the prestige of the priesthood. Augustine's victory over the Donatists resulted in the firm establishment of the seven sacraments that are still in force today within the Roman Catholic Church. The sacraments now accepted are baptism, communion, holy orders, confirmation, penance, marriage in the Church, and the last rights. Augustine had all Donatist churches and property turned over to the Roman church, and he denied that the Church was subject to the state.

During the next thirty years, Augustine labored successfully to establish a theological position in relation to the doctrine of the trinity and the free will of men. His success resulted in the Roman Church accepting the concept of three persons in the person of the human Christ, i.e., God, Christ and the Holy Spirit. In the end, Augustine accepted the position that Adam's original sin forever tainted all mankind with evil and no amount of good works could remove the taint of that sin — only the freely given grace of God could remove it. This grace was offered to all men, through the death of Christ on the cross, but many would refuse to accept it. Free will, in the view of Augustine, was limited to the choice that each person makes in relation to accepting or not accepting the offer of grace. God, however, has known through all time what decision will be made by each individual person — God is omnipotent and therefore knows from the beginning everything that will happen, and it can only happen in the way that he knows it. This is the doctrine of predestination that was to play so large a role not only in the Roman Church but also in the later Protestant sects of Christianity. Augustine did not create the doctrine of original sin but through him it became one of the leading tenets of the Roman Church.

Pelagius, his most able opponent, countered with the idea that man was truly free to chose his path, and that God only gave us a guide to follow in the revelation of his law and commandments, the cleansing waters of baptism, the example of the saints and prophets, and the redeeming blood of Christ. He did not believe that God had created man as inherently evil, nor did he accept the concept of original sin. He held that each man would be punished for the sins that he actually committed and which he had freely chosen. His view was that good works throughout the lifetime of an individual could assure the individual a place in salvation. His views were, in the end, declared by the Roman Church to be heresy and were not adopted into the Roman Church theology. Instead, they accepted Augustine's view that human reason was weak and the only path to salvation was in the possession of the living God. The doctrines set forth by Augustine, and accepted by the Roman Church, are the supports that now justify the concepts of the sacraments, the infallibility of the pope, and the claim that the secular aspect of life is subject to the dictates of the Church. But Augustine and Pelagius both believed they were men of God and devoted their lives to correctly interpreting the scriptures.

The Eastern Orthodox Church did not accept the teachings of Augustine, partly because of his lack of training in the Greek intellectual heritage, and partly because the Eastern Church had already submitted to the power of the Byzantine state. The Eastern Orthodox Church remained outside of the arguments that were being fought in the developing Roman Church. A longer look at the Orthodox Church will be taken later. The teachings of Augustine would dominate the Roman Church during the whole period now under consideration.

The early leaders of the later Reformation movement, such as Wycliff, Hus, Luther, and Calvin, would all return to the teachings of Augustine in their Protestant creeds. Augustine also established the first monastery (the Augustine Order) in the West. It would serve as the model for most of the monasteries that were established in Europe. Unlike the monastic orders that dotted Africa and Syria, Augustine did not base his order on severe asceticism. Rather, he established a form of communism, focusing on charity, coupled with a dedication to work and learning; these are the basis of the monastic movement in Western Europe to this day.

The last of the four trends was the inundation of Western Europe by the less civilized peoples of the north and east. The ease with which the Roman Church was able to convert these new peoples to Christianity rested on the manner in which the Catholic Church had consolidated the practices of Rome. The worship of the pagan pantheon of gods and goddesses had been converted to an intimate and individual worship of the saints of the Church. The pagan statues of Isis and Jupiter were renamed as Mary and Jesus. The Roman Lupercatia, and the feast of Isis, became the feast of the nativity. The Roman Saturnalia was replaced by the celebration of Christmas and the floralia became the Pentecost. All Souls Day took the place of the rituals of Roman ancestor worship. The resurrection of Christ replaced the resurrection cults that had been imported into Rome from the Near East as the celebration of Easter. The pagan use of incense, music, lights, flowers, processions, and the vestments were all adapted to the rituals of the Church. It was easy for the new peoples entering the defeated Roman Empire to recognize and identify their own rituals with those of the Roman Church, and conversion became merely a matter of changing names.

What the Roman Church did not incorporate from the old pagan faiths was the joy of indulging the sensual nature and their joy in the use of human reason. Even much of the magic and superstition of the pagans was transferred to the Church through the acceptance of the miracles that were effected by the ascetics. One example was the use of a representation of the cross to ward off evil. The Roman Church did not accept the pagan practice of polygamy, instead making marriage one of the sacraments of the Church. In the process, abortion, adultery, and all sexual conduct outside of marriage became mortal sins. The laws of the Church did not condemn slavery; in fact, many of its edicts even supported the institution of slavery. Within the Church, however, the doctrine of the legal and moral equality of all men was accepted (although not, perhaps, exactly as we understand it today) and the Church received all classes into her communion. Slaves, however, could not be confirmed into the priesthood. All in all, the Roman Church gave up the stoicism taught by Augustine, and taught instead the ethic of kindliness, obedience, humility, patience, mercy, purity, chastity and the other virtues which have become such a large part of Christian theology. This theology was mainly used to soften the duties of Christianity for the masses while at the same time the leadership of the Church, at least initially, accepted the more stoical manner of living.

The first to fall to the inundation of peoples was Britain. Here, the Roman heritage had not taken a very deep root, as the Celtic peoples of Scotland,

Ireland, and Wales had never been under Roman control. When Roman troops were withdrawn from Britain and redeployed to protect the rest of the empire from invasion, the Britons were subject to takeover by the Celts. The Britons sought help from their brethren on the continent and called for the Saxons, Angels, and others to come to their aid. These peoples were located in the Netherlands and northern Germany and also had never been subjected to Roman rule. They came; but of course, they did not just help ward off the Celtic attacks but rather took control of the province of Britain themselves. Under the influence of the Saxons, what little Roman culture that had existed was quickly lost. The only real vestige of Roman rule that remained was the Catholicism that had been established among the Scots and Irish.

The provinces of central Italy, Spain, and France fell next to the Vandals, who continued their migration into northern Africa, destroying Roman power bases in those areas. In Italy, the Ostrogoths (eastern Goths), who had been sent by the Eastern Emperor to retake the province, replaced the Vandals. The Ostrogoths had already accepted Christianity after being moved into Byzantine territory to protect it from migrations from the East. The Ostrogoths also controlled a large portion of the western Balkans, and Bohemia, Hungary, and a portion of Austria. Under the pressure applied by the Ostrogoths, the Visigoths (western Goths) moved further south and west, taking control of southern France and Spain, replacing the Vandals in this area. The Franks, a related people, took control of northern France and the areas of Alsace-Lorraine and parts of Switzerland.

In these areas, the existing population was largely Roman in cultural attributes, and gradually absorbed the new peoples into there way of life. These provinces were better organized and were still administered by the remaining Roman aristocracy. The new peoples mixed freely with the Roman aristocracy and adopted most of their administrative, economic and social customs. Regional varieties of the Latin language continued to be spoken in the provinces of France and Spain, where it gradually developed evolved into the hybrid languages of Spanish and French. Most of central and northern Europe, with the exception of England and Scandinavia, spoke various dialects of German. All of these peoples accepted Christianity as their religion; some (such as the Visigoths and Franks) completely, and others (such as the Vandals) less so. The Vandals were converted, due to the efforts of Augustine prior to his death. In Italy, the population was totally Roman in culture and Catholic in religion. The Ostrogoths were unable to change this and slowly became essentially Romanized; they lost the early start they had received in Orthodox theology.

Over the next 500 years the migrations settled down and each of these peoples settled in and established territories based on the language spoken and customs that they brought with them. This was the basis of the later evolution of nation states in Europe — the concept of the nation state was largely based upon the division of Europe into different language and custom groupings. The first to consolidate political power was the Roman Catholic Church, with the establishment of the Vatican and the surrounding areas as the seat of their religious and political power. From this base the Roman Catholic Church was able to spread its political influence into the rest of Europe and establish its clergy as the administrators of most of the secular governments then found in Europe.

The eastern portions of the Roman Empire did not suffer as complete destruction as the west. There were several reasons for this, the first being the incorporation of the Ostrogoths into the Balkans through land grants and the employment of these tribes as a bulwark against further incursions in that area. The strength of Sassanid Persia also kept the migrations of eastern peoples directed towards southern Russia and the Crimea rather than southward and westward into Byzantium. The new peoples were, however, able to take control of the areas once controlled by the Byzantines around the Black Sea. The Near East (due to the strength of the Byzantine Empire, and that of the Sassanids), was left essentially free from these migrations. The Sassanids, taking advantage of the problems in the west, established themselves in Syria, Palestine, and Egypt. They also pushed a short distance into the southern portions of modern Turkey. On the eastern end of the Sassanid Empire, they were forced to incorporate new peoples into their territories to help stem continuing migrations. In both the Byzantine and Sassanid Empires the constant warfare, pressure of migrating peoples, and cost of maintaining the luxury that they had become accustomed to, slowly depleted their will to survive and their treasury.

The Eastern Church, while differing little from the Western Church in theology, differed greatly in the case of ritual and administration. The most persistent disagreement that kept the two churches separated, and therefore on different paths of evolution, was the controversy over the nature of Christ. The Western Church had accepted as part of its creed that the person of Christ was consubstantial, i.e., both God and co-eternal with God. The Eastern Church adopted the creed that Christ was a part of God but was not co-eternal with him. This led to several distinctions in the ritual of the Church, such as the manner in which the sign of the cross was signified by the priests. All efforts at settling this difference of theology failed and the two churches remained separated on this issue.

Perhaps that was not the main issue; of more importance was the fact that the Eastern Church had already submitted itself to the domination of the state. This meant that they were administered differently. In the West, the Pope was supreme and could not be challenged even by the secular ruler. In the East, the Emperor was supreme even in the Church and he appointed the chief administrative officers of the Church. This also resulted in a much more elaborate ceremonial structure within the Church, as the dignity of the state was also at stake. The pressure on the Byzantine state to maintain its independence also caused the classes in that society to become much more rigid than in the West. As a result, the Eastern Church was much less able to recruit talented men from all levels of society. Maybe the most important administrative consequence was that the emperor, as head of the Church, was also able to directly involve himself in the drafting and issuing of religious edicts. The last, but not least, difference that kept the Churches separated was the conversion of the Eastern Church from Latin to Greek as the official language of the Church. The differences were great enough over a period of time to result in the first real division of Christianity into the Roman Catholic and Greek Orthodox sects. The latter branch later developed several subsets, including the Russian, Bulgarian and Romanian Orthodox Churches.

This was essentially the position held by both the Sassanid and Byzantine empires at the time of the birth of Islam and its subsequent growth in political power. Byzantium's role vis-à-vis the West then changed from that of an antagonist, a rival for control of the empire, to that of a relatively peaceful neighbor and important buffer. For some seven centuries, the Byzantine Empire was to block Islam from penetrating into the lands of Europe and was to be the reason for the relatively peaceful period of time that allowed for the growth of the nation-state system.

We now turn to the birth of Islam as a religion and to its subsequent spread and development in the Near East, Africa, Central Asia, and the Far East. Islam spread phenomenally quickly after its foundation by Mohammad in Arabia. Within a very short time, his generals moved out into the Near East and took the weakened Empire of the Sassanids, which included Iran, Iraq, Afghanistan, Pakistan, and portions of Central Asia. They also were able to easily overrun the areas now contained in Syria, Lebanon, Israel, Egypt, and the territories controlled by the Berbers in North Africa. They extended their conquests into the southern portions of modern Turkey. This gave them control of all of the vast caravan trade of the Near East and Central Asia. The Byzantine Empire was able to hang on to the waterway trade routes of the Black Sea and the eastern Mediterranean trade. On the far western end of their empire, the Muslims gained control of Sicily and Spain. They quickly consolidated their control over this vast area by adopting wholesale the techniques of administration, commercial trade, finance, and legal control that they had found in Persia. They established Islam as the official religion, but adopted the Persian tradition of tolerance for the customs and religion of other peoples. This policy was largely responsible for a long period of relative peace that followed their takeover of this vast empire.

The religion of Islam is essentially the work of one man, the prophet Mohammad. The word Islam in Arabic means "to surrender" or "to make peace" and the word Moslem, or Muslim, is commonly translated as "the ones who surrender." Mohammad was born into and was raised as a member of the tribe Hashim, a part of the larger clan known as Quraish, who controlled the city of Mecca. Mohammad was raised in the presence of both Christians and Jews, but seems to have maintained closer contact with the Jewish people in the area. His knowledge of the Old Testament and the Talmud was extensive.

As with Judaism, there is no separation of the secular and religious in Islam. Mohammad based Islam on the belief that he was the last in a long line of prophets sent by God to teach mankind his will. This line of prophets had begun with Adam and included Moses, Jesus Christ and the other Old Testament prophets. He accepted as the divine words of God both the Old and New Testaments, the first as delivered to Moses, and the latter as delivered to Jesus. He believed, however, that both of these bodies of writing had been corrupted by the later development of Judaic and Christian theology. His mission was to cleanse the corruption from the word of God and return mankind to the true path of righteousness.

Tradition states that one night, about 610 AD, Mohammad was alone in a cave on his return from a business trip and the angel Gabriel appeared to him and told him to read the inscription on his night shirt. Mohammad was unable to read and questioned the order of the angel. He was made to understand the inscription and was attempting to leave the cave when Gabriel appeared again, calling to him, "O Mohammad! Thou art the messenger of Allah and I am Gabriel." This was repeated one more time as Mohammad left the cave. Allah appears to have been the chief god of the clan Quraish. The religion of this clan also included angels, Jinn (demons) and the god of evil, Iblis. The angels, the Jinn, and Iblis, although supernatural, were higher forms of life but were not truly divine. They were in fact subject to Allah, just as humans were. Mohammad adopted all of these into the new religion of Islam.

Mohammad continued the development of Islam through a continuing series of revelations covering a period of some 23 years. Mohammad did not write down any of his own revelations, but others wrote down the revelations as they occurred and placed the records in safekeeping. There were also others who had memorized all of the revelations of Mohammad.

The ancient sacred site of the Quraish was the Kaaba that centered on a large black stone. Mohammad eventually adopted this site as the site that symbolized the religion of Islam. It was the spot to which all Moslems were required to turn in prayer and today is still the direction in which prayer is offered. The sacred site of the Kaaba is located in the city of Mecca, which now became the holiest city in Islam. Medina (the city in which Mohammad had found refuge from the Quraish and had given birth to Islam) and Jerusalem (the holy city of Abraham, from whom the Quraish believed they were descended) also became holy cities for the religion of Islam.

Upon arriving in Medina, after being forced out of Mecca by the leaders of the Quraish in response to his growing popularity, or rather the growing popularity of Islam, he was greeted with a show of affection. Tradition holds that people everywhere in the city of Medina were trying to get him to stop and were even holding the bridle of his camel. He answered them by saying that the camel would decide the stopping place and that the camel should be allowed to travel freely. This simple statement allayed their jealousy and left the decision to the will of Allah. At the point at which the camel stopped, Mohammad built his first mosque (the Islamic Church or Temple) and also a couple of buildings for his family.

Tradition says that at the first meeting held at the mosque, Mohammad climbed to the pulpit with his back to the congregation and said with a loud voice, "Allah is most great." The congregation followed suit and mouthed the same words. Mohammad, with his back still to the crowd, backed out of the pulpit after saying a prayer; and when he reached the foot of the alter, prostrated himself three times. In this prostration arose the symbolization of submitting one's soul to Allah. Hence the name Islam or Moslem. Mohammad then asked the congregation to honor that ritual for all time. The service then ended with a sermon which, in the case of Mohammad, was always an additional revelation from Allah.

As a prophet, the authority accorded to him began at the same time to devolve civil power onto him. The revelations of Mohammad were not just religious pronouncements but also touched on the personal morals, finance, agriculture, hygiene, and many other aspects of the daily life of Moslems. The revelations, being seen as the divine word of God, were accorded the force of sacred laws.

Shortly after the death of Mohammad, the few men who had memorized all of his revelations began also to die off and others were not replacing them. Soon, the accounts of the revelations began to vary from place to place. In AD 633, the caliph Abu Bekr ordered that all the revelations be brought together and be written down. A man named Zaid ibn Thabit, who had also been Mohammad's chief diary writer, accomplished the task of writing down the revelations. The resulting book, which like the Hebrew Talmud had no vowels, soon began to be corrupted by those who interpreted it through public reading. A revision was ordered by caliph Othman and was made by the same Zaid. Official copies of this book were sent to Damascus, Kufa, and Basra, the three main centers of Islamic learning. Since that time the book, which became known as the Qur'an, has been maintained with exceptional purity. It is without a doubt the most accurate rendition of an ancient religion that exists today. The Qur'an clearly displays its debt to Judaism in many of its taboos, religious laws, and the concern for the civil law.

The revelations of Mohammad owe a large share of their content to similar or identical passages in the Old Testament or the Talmud. This, however, is not really surprising as Mohammad accepted without question that these documents also contained the revealed word of God. Mohammad accepted the strict monotheism of Judaism and considered the concept of the Christian Trinity as a concession to polytheism. He also adopted many of the rules of hygiene and ritual that were practiced in Judaism.

Islam differed from Judaism mainly in the fact that Mohammad believed that he was the long awaited Messiah of the Jews. They rejected him as the Messiah just as they had rejected Jesus Christ, although some may have accepted him as a prophet.

The Qur'an also shows some debt to the Christian and Zoroastrian religions, but by far its greatest debt is to Judaism. In addition many of the traditional beliefs of the Arabs were incorporated into the Qur'an, such as the Jihad, or holy war, polygamy, slavery, and a secular commercial acumen that had developed over centuries of operating the caravan trade. The Qur'an, like the Talmud, makes law and morals one and the same. In the Qur'an, one can find rules on manners, hygiene, marriage and divorce, the treatment of children, the treatment of slaves and animals; there are also rules of conduct for commerce, politics, finance, war and peace, and many others. As with Judaism, Islam is the day-to-day, face-to-face, meeting of Moslems with their god. Islam gave to its adherents, and those around, the simplest, least mystical, least ritualistic of all existing religions. It was essentially free from idolatry and sacerdotalism (reliance upon the priesthood) and it elevated the moral and ethic behavior of the believers while at the same time promoting social order and unity. It tended to disarm superstition and magic, and promised eternal happiness to the believers. In general, its adherents were more stoical and tolerant than their counterparts in Christian lands. Unfortunately, this last trait has not been completely brought forward to the current day.

All in all, the religion of Islam was one that could easily be accepted by the adherents of either Judaism or Christianity, as could be expected of a religion that was created to correct the perceived corruption of these two religions. Christians and Jews were, in fact, invited to convert to Islam, while at the same time they were allowed to practice their religion without molestation. Most Jews and Christians declined the offer, initially, but many would later join the Islamic faith. The stumbling block in each case has been a lack of ability of Christians and Jews to accept Mohammad as a prophet and the Qur'an as the revealed word of God. By the year AD 700, Islam had arrived at the basic form it retains to this day. Several minor changes have been made to the original tenets, such as the practice of secluding women, and several different movements have grown in importance within the general community. Some of these later branches are the ones that are gaining the most attention in today's world.

During the next four centuries, Islamic scholars spent their time collecting the sayings and the actions of the prophet and other leading figures of Islam into the Hadith (which is a collection of the thoughts and actions of the prophet, and other leading figures, written in book form). Four major schools developed during this process, absorbing all others, and collectively came to represent orthodox Islam, which is known as Sunni. The schools are the Hanafi (now found only in Sa'udi Arabia, it is considered to be the most fundamental and uncompromising of the four schools), the Malic'i (also a very rigid traditionalist school, it is found now mostly in Africa), the Shafic'i (essentially a Hadith, or a collection of sayings and actions, rather than a school of thought; it is found today in Egypt, and Yemen, and it is the only school that is found in the Far East) and the Hanbali (found today in Turkey, Syria, Central Asia, Afghanistan, Pakistan, and India. It is generally considered to the most practical of all the schools in its approach to Islam). One of the questions that face Islam today concerns how much, and what part, of the four schools of thought, or law, should be included within a modern Islamic state.

During the same period, and for sometime afterwards, another approach to Islam evolved. This sect suggested that the fusion of the secular and religious life in Islam was an error, and sought the more mystical aspects of Islam. They were known by the name of Sufis, and initially they seem to have called for a legalist doctrine, similar to the other schools. They were very much fundamentalist in their call for a return to the simple faith of the Qur'an. Their emphasis on the direct religious experience brought them into conflict with the major traditional schools of thought. The Sufis were the great missionaries of Islam, as their interpretation of the Qur'an was the most pleasing to the peoples of Central Asia, India and the Far East. Many of the Sufis were also ascetics, and wherever they went, the practice followed them. They seem to have been the stimulus that has led to the modern doctrine of the Shiite sect (a dissident sect of Islam opposed to the Sunni).

Within Islam, unlike the other major religions of the time, the tradition that developed around its growth was not devoted to theology but rather the law. The concept of divine law is as old as organized religion in the Near East, especially in relation to Judaism, but it was approached differently in Islam. Within Islam, the law has two major sources, the Qur'an and the Hadiths of the four legalist schools. In the Qur'an, Allah appears as the one who commands and prohibits the various actions of mankind expressed in the revelations of Mohammad. Allah is also the one who rewards and punishes any observance or disobedience to his commands, as given in the Qur'an. The Hadiths are the law concerning the actions and example of the Prophet. From the beginning, the

111

Hadiths were a major source of the right actions and thoughts which were required by traditional Islam in the day to day practice of Islam.

As mentioned above, the Christian Church had a model at hand — the Roman secular legal system — when it took over the governmental duties of the defunct Western Roman Empire. Islam did not have at its disposal a ready-made set of secular laws when it started its conquests. It was not until it had completely absorbed and adapted the older traditions of the Sassanids that this type of legal system was developed. This source was also found wanting, as Islam did not separate secular life from religious life, or at least Islam tended to fuse the two aspects of life to an even greater degree than the Sassanids, who also tended to combine religious and civil life into one system. Over the next four centuries the scholars of Islam, as a response to the Sassanid separation of civil and religious law, created the four legal schools to adapt the Persian religious and secular law to the use of the Moslems. The result was the development of Sunni or traditional Islam.

The Islamic word for the legal system is Shari'a, or "The Way," and appears to have been a later development from the word Fiqh, or understanding of the law. Initially, this concept was limited in scope to the model whereby Allah speaks and commands, and the believer submits and obeys. Obedience, in Islam, is not at all similar to the concept of "obedience" as it is understood in Christianity. In the Christian tradition, obedience to the law is somewhat passive and servile, while in Islam it is looked upon as a positive religious experience to be undertaken actively and with joy. the Sufis made some protest against this emphasis on the law; they felt that it would undermine the spiritual aspects of Islam. In the end, the legalist position won the debate and the four schools have become so firmly established that they control all aspects of the life of the believer. They have also since that time been expanded to control all aspects of the manner in which non-Moslems are to be governed and treated.

The four schools which have developed within the traditional system are intended to prescribe how their adherents are to perform their religious duties (ritual) and how they will interpret the law itself. Each school differs somewhat on just how religious duties are to be approached and how the law is to be interpreted. The main point to be made is that, whatever school, or tradition, the believer belongs to, he is acting within the confines of traditional Islam and is accepted as being a accepted part of the faith.

Although some parallels can be drawn between the four schools and the sectarian divisions of Christianity, they do not seem to be valid analogies. Even in the case of the Roman Catholic and Greek Orthodox Churches, the differences were emphasized to the exclusion of the similarities. This is even more clearly observed in the case of the Catholic and Protestant Churches. In the case of the four legal schools of Islam, the exact opposite is true, in other words, the similarities were emphasized to the point that all of them could be accepted as correct ways to interpret the law of Islam. This division of views between the four schools today is the issue most widely debated in Islam. The debate centers around what part of the thought of the four schools and just how much of each should be included within the framework of the modern Islamic state. Each school has a center of influence within Islam that relates to one of the modern states, or regions, as set forth above. These areas of influence should be considered when a reaction to the policies of these areas is formulated.

The Hanbali school was founded as a protest against the rationalist school (Mu'tazila). This rationalist school of thought had entered into Islam presumably through its contact with the classical traditions found in Roman and Greek thought centered in Alexandria and Constantinople. One of the tenets of the rationalists was that the Qur'an was not directly the divine word, but had rather been created by Allah as a guide to following Allah's commands. The Hanbali school has therefore based its interpretations of the law on a very fundamentalist view. The Hanbali school tends to reject any statement, or thought, that is not capable of being solidly placed in either the Qur'an or the Hadith used by the school itself. The Hanbali school is considered to be the most severe and uncompromising school within the practice of traditional Islam. As mentioned earlier this school today is found only in Saudi Arabia.

The Maliki school today is located mainly in Northern Africa, including Upper Egypt and was also the main school that was found in Moslem Spain. This school is also seen as a very severe system of traditional belief, with the addition of a very strong tradition of uncritical acceptance of authority. This last aspect may be part of the fascination of the learned scholars of this school with the thought of Aristotle and other Greek thinkers of the "scientific" schools. This school was the one with which the Normans, who had taken control of Sicily and Southern Italy came into contact with on a large scale basis. It is also the school which the missionaries being sent out by the monasteries of Western Europe came into contact with in Spain. It was from this school that most of Europe received its initial introduction to Islam and Islamic thought

The Shafi'I, as we have seen, tended to take a middle road between the rationalist approach and personal interpretation of the law. Today, this school is mainly found in Lower Egypt, Southern Arabia, Central Asia, and the Far East. It is a major influence on nationalist movements in both Central Asia and the Far East. As a result, today, it seems to be becoming somewhat more parochial in thought and action in these areas.

The Hanafi School is traditionally seen as the school most deeply involved in the rationalist philosophy and the most logical of the schools. As the official interpreter of the law for both the Ottoman and Mughal empires, this school was involved in the more practical problems of government as well as the questions of theology. As a result, this school presents a wider view than the other schools and tends to be more flexible in its beliefs. This school represents the other major point of contact with Europe during the reawakening of Europe to the classical traditions of Greece during the period of Europe's reawakening to classical thought during the Renaissance. This was particularly true of the trading cities of Italy and the Crusaders who sacked Constantinople in AD 1204.

For those who wish to look deeper into the specific differences between the four schools, the reading list in Appendix A should provide ample material. The last aspect of Islam to be touched upon is the Pilgrimage (Hajj). The pilgrimage is a system whereby every believer who can goes to Mecca at the same time of year and they all interact with one another in equality. Thousands come each year to demonstrate their belief in the brotherhood of all adherents of Islam. At these meetings, they are allowed to exchange ideas and experiences as well as obtain all the latest books. The fact that Islam has been able to incorporate the four schools into one traditional system testifies to the effectiveness of this tradition in binding the believers of Islam into one body.

Up until this point, we have concentrated on the Sunni, or traditional, segment of Islam, which represents the vast majority of believers. There is, however, a strong tradition of sects that believe themselves to be outside the traditional system. It is here that one might be able to make a valid comparison with sectarian Christianity. The origin of this tradition of dissent began very early in the history of Islam. It began with the murder of the second leader of Islam (the first after Muhammad), Umar. The companions, after much debate, decided upon the election of Uthman. He was the son-in-law of Muhammad and was also connected to the leading family of Mecca, which had initially opposed Muhammad. In electing Uthman, the companions neglected the claim of Ali — who was also the son-in-law and cousin of Muhammad. Ali's followers revolted against the rule of Uthman in the eleventh year of his reign. Uthman was murdered during this revolt, and Ali was offered, and accepted, the leadership. This brought about a moral conflict within Islam that has not been resolved to this day. The conflict centers on the belief that it is wrong to accept the murder of Uthman; but it is also wrong to accept the actions that led to the revolt against Uthman. Even taking a neutral position, in this case, is wrong.

This is the basis upon which all dissenting schools within Islam are founded. The leaders of the revolt against Uthman also revolted against the rule of Ali. Mu'awija somehow convinced Ali to accept arbitration of the dispute between himself and the leaders of the revolt. The result, from a political point of view, was that Mu'awija, and his house (known as the Umayya) ruled Islam for the next ninety years. From a religious point of view the leaders of the revolt considered Ali to have committed an act of apostasy in the acceptance of arbitration. The Qur'an clearly states that those who rebel should not be allowed to compromise. They separated themselves from the Islamic community and created a new sect known as Kharijis. The faction which had supported Ali also set themselves up as a new sect known as the Shi'I. The Kharijis were totally uncompromising in their stand against traditional Islam and over time were eliminated, with the exception of one more moderate branch known as Ibadis. The various wars of the Kharijis were a real source of terror for most Muslims and seem to be the first real use of the Jihad or holy war, at least in relation to one group of Muslims warring against another group of Muslims. The Ibadis branch found its center of influence in Northern Africa, especially Algeria, where it set up an independent state. This state was later destroyed by the Shi'I state of Tunisia. The Kharijis are few in number today and are found mainly in Zanzibar and Libya. The follows of this sect still consider themselves to be the only real Muslims. They are the most puritanical of all the sects that hold themselves to be outside the traditional Islamic faith.

In modern terms, it should be remembered that the Shi'ites are considered by the traditional arm of Islam to be true believers — but believers with a theology that is not essentially correct. This has allowed the conduct of holy war between the two branches without either being outside the Islamic community. This situation to a large degree still remains in effect today.

In the case of the Shi'ites, who also fight against the improprieties of the Sunni, the Sunni are not considered to be non-Muslims but rather as Muslims who have strayed from the true path laid out in the Qur'an and the Hadiths. They are not as uncompromising in their war with the traditional branch and have survived in much larger numbers than the Kharijis. The largest of the Shi'ite sects are located in Iran, Iraq, southern Lebanon, and India. In theological issues they are rationalist in thought and believe that the Qur'an was created. They see Allah as good and incapable of doing anything evil. Allah left the Qur'an with Muhammad as a rational guide for mankind in his attempt to follow the law. Mankind was created with free will, however, and through the use of reason can freely chose to follow or not follow the commandments of Allah. They also believe that various holy men or Imams have been sent by Allah to further help mankind keep to the path of righteousness. The 12th Imam that was sent did not die but was taken to Allah in much the same way that Jesus was, in the Christian belief. This Imam will return at the last judgment and claim the true believers of Islam. In the practice of Islam, the Shi'ite tend to be strict fundamentalists.

It must also be remembered that the idea of the holy war was from the beginning intended to apply to non-believers. There is, however (as one might imagine) some difference in the method and the manner in which the concept of Jihad can be used against non-believers.

Later we will attempt to set forth the manner in which Atheism might approach the question of Islam in the modern world, in particular, the response of the United States to the attack on the World Trade Center. First, we will trace the further development of religious and secular thought in Europe and the United States. Particular attention will be paid to the foundations of modern Atheism.

Chapter 5. Modern Religious Thought and the Birth of Atheism

We have reached the point where the three religions that have had the largest effect upon the development of Western European civilization have been established in their modern form. It is now time to concentrate on the development of Europe during the period leading directly to our own time. It is here that we find the foundations of an atheism that will be recognized as a possible social force. It is also here that we can follow the weakening of Christianity and religion in general, for a short period of time.

Four major movements that together brought European civilization to its modern form marked the period between AD 1300 and 1900. They are, in order of their appearance the Renaissance (the reawakening of learning), the Reformation (the splintering of Christianity in Europe), the Enlightenment (the establishment of science and the nation-state), and the Industrial Revolution (the conversion of Europe from feudalism to a modern capital economy). The general movements within each of these will be looked at from the point of view of establishing the foundation for Part Two of this work, which discusses the role of atheism in modern society.

The Renaissance essentially revolves around the opening of the educated classes of Europe to the teachings of the ancient Greeks, Hellenes, Romans, Persians, Indians, and Egyptians. One irony of the Renaissance is that this reawakening of learning was the result of the intellectual scholarship of the educated classes within Judaism and Islam. Both of these religions developed a strong commitment to learning and the education of the adherents of their faith. They were equally committed to extending a tolerance to all learning and did not hesitate to study the knowledge of Greece, Rome, Egypt, and others. Unfortunately, the Christians they came into contact with over time rarely returned this tolerance.

The scholars of Judaism had translated most of the Greek classics into their own language of Hebrew. They had found much of this knowledge in the libraries of Constantinople and Alexandria, where large communities of Jewish people had settled earlier. The sack of Constantinople in the year AD 1204 by the Christian crusaders later destroyed many of the works that these scholars had translated from the original Greek.

The scholars of Islam were much more broadly based, as they not only translated the Greek classics but also those of Persia, India, and Egypt into Arabic. The scholars of Islam unfortunately concentrated on the translation of later Greek works involving neo-Platonism and Neo-Pythagoreanism, although they did translate some of the classical works, such as some of Aristotle's works. In the case of the scholars of Islam an additional treat was in store for Europe. They, in their efforts to find the "philosopher's stone" that would allow them to convert base metals to gold, had established the field of chemistry — the only example of true science that existed at that time. They had also gone far in the development of mathematics and many others fields of what today are known as the natural sciences. The actual method of transmission of this knowledge is now unknown to us, but much of it was physically taken and carried to the West by the crusaders who sacked the Eastern Capital in AD 1204. In this case, the actual Greek and Roman manuscripts themselves were brought to the West and deposited in the monasteries that were scattered in various countries. The Italian city-states had also begun to dominate trade in the Mediterranean region, and that would put them in direct contact with both the Byzantines and Moslems. In addition, the various monasteries of Europe were sending missionaries into Spain in an attempt to convert the Muslims to Christianity. This opened them to the work of scholars such as Averroes, Avicenna, and Maimonides.

The pillaging of Constantinople had weakened the Byzantine Empire to the point that they were unable to maintain their control over trade in the eastern Mediterranean region. Initially, they called upon the city-state of Venice for support, but soon Venice had established a virtual monopoly on this trade. At about the same time, the Normans (descendents of the original Vikings who had taken control of Northern France) took control of the western Mediterranean by conquering Sicily and southern Italy. The Norman invaders — for a period of about 100 years — controlled the trade between Italy, North Africa, Spain, and France and both the Byzantine Empire and the Islamic peoples of the Near East. This shifting of trade from the older cultures to the Europeans had two major effects. The first, and maybe the more important, was the increase in wealth and independence of the city-states of Italy and the Normans, who controlled the island of Sicily and portions of Southern Italy.. With all their wealth, they could operate essentially free of interference from the Roman Catholic Church. The second result was the close contact between the Normans and the Moslems in both Sicily and Spain, and the contact between the Venetians and scholars of Byzantine origin. Both tended to develop a skeptical attitude towards Christianity and settled into an aristocratic support of scholars under their pay.

As the knowledge of Greek and Roman heritage passed throughout Europe, a skeptical attitude towards religion began to appear, especially in the northern city-states of Italy, among the Normans, and in Germany. "Heresies" began to appear, led by such men as Wycliff, Hus, and others, and within the Church itself in the writings of Thomas Aquinas. The skepticism and heresies that appeared can be traced to the contact with Islamic and Judaic scholars. Thomas Aquinas is probably the most representative of the effects of the Renaissance. Aquinas was well acquainted with the work of Averroes, Avicenna, Maimonides, and many others. He had also studied and imbibed the work of Aristotle, as had those above.

Through his efforts, although he at first was treated as a heretic, the doctrines of the Roman Catholic Church were converted from the influence of Augustine to those of scholasticism. The main effort of Aquinas was to accommodate reason to the religious theology of his time — or vice versa. He did this by simply stating that the basic tenets of Christianity were not subject to reason and must be accepted as an act of faith alone. All of the rest of religious theology, he subjected to reason, and began the movement known as scholasticism. He accepted the notion of predestination, as presented by Augustine, but in nearly every other area it was a victory of Aristotle over Augustinian mysticism. He represents the first attempt at higher criticism in relation to the scriptures and the theology of Christianity.

After Aquinas, mainly through the efforts of Duns Scotus, it was shown that reason could not establish the foundation of religion, and scholasticism was shattered. This so weakened the Church that a later revolt broke out along doctrinal and ecclesiastical lines. The result of this revolt was most clearly seen in France, Germany, and northern Italy in their stout resistance not only to the religious domination of the Church, but also to its domination of secular life. In particular, the abuses that had crept into the use of the sacraments were pointed out by these men — who were called heretics. At this early date the heresies that appeared were not aimed at the reform of the Church but rather only at pointing out the errors that the Church had fallen into. The identification and highlighting of these errors was supported by the higher criticism initiated by Aquinas. Within these early heresies can be found all the tenets (that appeared in force some two or three centuries later) that were to justify the Reformation movement. In the case of the Normans located in Sicily and Southern Italy, in particular, can also be found all the principles which later led to the formation of the nation-state system that was to be one of the major hallmarks of European civilization. The Normans who settled in this area established the first government in Italy that completely separated the functions of government and religion. The Renaissance can be seen as the slow adoption and incorporation of Judaic and Islamic development of early Greek thought into the grasp of the educated classes of Europe, especially their adoption and further development of Greek thought in the areas of medicine, biology, chemistry (the first true use of the scientific method), astronomy, and the other natural sciences.

The Catholic Church initially stoutly fought these movements, particularly with the use of the Inquisition. This rigid and inflexible response was very effective in the short run and in a period of three centuries nearly exterminated the reform movements directed towards the Church, and the development of independent states. The acceptance of the teachings of Thomas Aquinas into the theology of the Church and the reform efforts of the monastic movement in general may have been a major factor in the long-term failure of the reactionary response of the Church. The monastic movement, under the influence of scholasticism, gave up its concern with worldly affairs and for awhile concentrated on the spiritual improvement of mankind. They went back to the simplicity of early Christianity and brought to the towns and villages higher standards of agricultural technique, financial responsibility, and higher standards of personal moral and ethical behavior. Although this movement was accepted and used by the Church for its own purposes, it was not effective in changing the attitudes and ways of the higher clergy and aristocratic classes of the population. In short, this reform movement brought the Church again to the leadership of both secular and religious affairs for another three centuries. The city-states of northern Italy and the still living heresies that found haven in Germany were the only active resistance to be found against the Church at this time.

The second movement began about AD 1450, when the papacy was taken over by the French secular state. The Roman Church had been unable to sustain its start toward self-reform had fallen back into its earlier abuses of the sacraments and secular power. The general disorganization of the Holy Roman Empire, centered in Germany, coupled with renewed attacks on the Byzantine Empire by the forces of Islam, and the fall of North Africa to the Moors, forced the Roman Catholics to seek the protection of France. The seat of papal power was moved to France for a period of some 68 years. During this period of time, France was at war with England, and Italy and Germany resented the Church's move to France and the resultant control of church administrative posts by French nationals. The English, in particular, resented the flow of cash from England through the sale of indulgences and benefices. They felt that this money was being used largely for the support of the French war effort against England. The people of Italy and Germany also resented the outflow of cash from their territories into France. During this relatively short period, all of the tenets and frustrations that led to the Reformation came to the forefront.

An additional factor that led to the Reformation was the great wealth that was beginning to flow into Europe from the great trading empires that were being built by Spain and Portugal. The business classes in Germany, in particular, began to develop a strong sense of cohesion and began to demand the relaxation of secular control by the aristocratic class, to which the Catholic secular administrators belonged. They also demanded the relaxation of religious strictures against commercial activities that had been adopted by the Catholic

Church in its theology. The opening of the trade route around Africa to India and the Far East was a true all-water trade route. It destroyed the Mediterranean monopoly of trade with the East and weakened the once wealthy Italian city-states. It was the main reason that the Renaissance came to an end. The Spanish, in their attempt to bypass the Portuguese monopoly on trade with the East, discovered the Americas and brought an abundance of gold and silver into the European markets. In addition the fall of the Byzantine Empire to Islam, in AD 1453, caused the shift of the Central Asian trade routes northward to the German cities located in Bohemia, Austria, and Hungary — that is, cities built by German settlers in neighboring countries. In short, the wealth that had for thousands of years been centered in the Near East and Turkey now slowly found a new center in Europe. This new wealth was largely responsible for the growth of truly independent nation-states within Europe, first in Spain, Portugal, and France, and later in England, Holland, Scandinavia and Denmark. This process was occurring at the same time as the Reformation and the new states used the new Christian creeds in their war against the secular control of the Roman Church. The fall of Byzantium and the consequent conquest of the Balkans by Islam created a problem that still faces the world today. Under the Byzantine influence these areas were Christian in religion, but with the coming of Islam a large segment of the population converted to Islam. This was not surprising, as the Greek Orthodox Church had for centuries been dominated by the state and the people were inculcated to a system in which there was no separation of religion and the secular life. The conversion to Islam was to be seen, in particular, in Croatia, Serbia, Bosnia, and other southern Balkan states. Even in areas, such as Bulgaria and Greece where the population remained heavily Christian, the Moslems established powerful communities. By AD 1500, therefore, all of the factors were in place — even the newly invented printing press — for the development of the Reformation.

The Reformation began in Germany under the leadership of Martin Luther. It is of some importance to understand the political situation in Germany if we mean to have any understanding of the Reformation. The German lands were divided into at least three major types of political associations. There were, first and foremost, the lands and manors of the aristocrats who represented the manpower of the Holy Roman Empire. They were largely semi-independent feudal agricultural estates paying homage to the Elector, whom the Pope appointed to rule the Empire. This type of structure incorporated the majority of the population of Germany as we know it today. The second type was found in the major cities and towns of Germany. Here factors, such as trade, had created a middle class of businessmen, they held control of the administration of the local governments. Generally, they also acknowledged the supremacy of the Empire and Pope in matters both secular and religious, but on the secular side they exercised a greater independence than even the feudal lords in relation to the Elector. The third type of organization was found in the semi-independent kingdoms of Austria, Bohemia, and Hungary. Here, the administration was under the control of lords who acknowledged the Holy Roman Empire but who acted as if the empire did not exist. In short, there was no unifying power in the empire that extended to these areas and a resort to war normally settled all disputes. Nominally, the whole structure was subject to the religious dictates of the Roman Church and the Catholic clergy actually held the most important administrative posts.

In his efforts to reform the Church, Luther became persecuted and was forced to seek the protection of German nationalists, which was largely centered in the business class of the major cities. The concept of German nationalism had already taken hold of the middle classes of the cities and in the eastern lands of Austria, Bohemia, and Hungary. The latter had already produced the heresies of John Hus and the Waldenites. Both of these heretical movements continued to exist in these areas and followed much the same creed as that of Luther. It is difficult, in fact, to determine how much of Luther's doctrine was borrowed from these earlier movements

Luther initially attacked the Roman Church only in an attempt to reform its abuses in the use of the sacraments and the sale of religious posts. The Church had forsworn its earlier attempts at reform; presumably, because it was unwilling to give up the income, which, to be sure, in part allowed it to continue its widespread secular activities, and certainly because the Catholic administrative officials refused to give up their vested interests, including the status, power and comfort that this income gave them. Luther's initial stance denied the power of the priest to change the bread of the Eucharist into the actual body of Christ. Instead, he claimed, the most that could be believed was that Christ was present only through his grace and that the actual bread remained. Luther also interpreted the gospels to show that both wine and bread should be used to celebrate the Eucharist. The Roman Church had stopped using wine in the ritual, as they said, for fear of "spilling the blood of Christ." (Maybe, also, for reasons of economy?) Luther also denied the power of the priest, and even the pope, to forgive the sins of man through the private confession and penance. At most, the Church could only forgive man the sins that he committed in this world and ask for God's mercy in the world to come. In Luther's view, the forgiveness of sins was the sole responsibility of God through the exercise of his grace. Luther was persecuted by the Church for these views, and was sentenced to death. He sought the protection of the German nationalists and received it, nullifying the papal edict, in effect.

Luther, now classified as a heretic, took a much stronger stand, basing his teaching solely on the scriptures. He denied the infallibility of the Pope, and established in place of that notion the notion of the freedom of each individual to interpret the scriptures for himself. Luther did accept the Augustinian concept of predestination, under which God was seen to have chosen, from the beginning, those who would receive grace and those who would not. Luther believed that the number of the elect would be very limited and that most people would be damned. It goes without saying that those who would be among the elect were those who believed as Luther did.

John Calvin, who was much more influential generally than Luther, had also taken up the torch of Reformation. Calvin's creed went by the name of the Reformed Church (a reformed version of Lutheranism). It was, in fact, only one of many creeds that soon appeared throughout Europe. This was to be expected when we take into consideration that one of the main tenets of the Protestant movement was each person's right to interpret the scriptures for himself. Calvin, however, was not attached to any national movement; God was his only country. Calvin also accepted the doctrine of predestination along with many of the Lutheran tenets. In addition, he added a very severe discipline similar to that of the early Christians.

As a result of the spreading of these ideas throughout Germany, the freedom to interpret the scriptures was coupled with the related freedom of choice in the selection of secular rulers. In this related belief we find the real beginning of the general movement towards removing clergy and aristocracy from the sole power of secular rule. The protection that was afforded to Luther by the barons and lords, as well as by the middle classes of the cities, was given mainly in furtherance of the effort to oust the Church from administrative roles inside the state. By the end of the 16th century, the ideas of Luther had spread throughout Europe, but because of its attachment to German nationalism the creed itself had little influence outside Germany.

Calvin's world was very gloomy indeed, compared even to Luther's. With Calvin the Renaissance and Reformation both came to an end. Calvin and his followers were specifically averse to learning in all its forms, with the sole exception of the scriptures. They even, at times, advocated that parents not educate their children in any way except for knowledge of the scriptures. His faith was based upon a call to return to the simple asceticism of the primitive

Christians. As a result, he was extremely intolerant of those who did not believe as he did. By the time of his death, Calvin's creed had spread throughout France (the Huguenots), Spain, Holland, England (the Puritans), and portions of Germany that were not Lutheran. Calvin was clearly the most influential of the reformers both in organizational skill and theological foundation. As his ideas spread, they were mitigated to some degree in their severity to accommodate the needs of the people who converted to his creed. The doctrine of predestination was relaxed and now included a much larger number of people, even some of the more noble of the pagans. It was now possible, under Calvin's creed, for the number of the elect to be expanded by the simple means of conversion to Protestant belief. Many of his severe restrictions on dress, dancing, make-up, prayer, church attendance, and social activities were also softened greatly. Some groups, however, such as the Puritans, tended to maintain the creed in most of its severity. With the doctrine espoused by Calvin, and its later development, the rigid concept of predestination was converted to the concept of universal salvation.

By the end of the 17th century, Protestantism had become what it is for us today: a highly fractured faith containing numerous creeds. They all accept the same basic beliefs but differ greatly in the method by which they practice these beliefs. Each has its own particular brand of organization, its own oddities of theological belief, and its own ritual. The basic tenets of Protestantism, however, stand in relief against those of the Roman Catholic Church. First and foremost is the belief that the Bible is the sole source of God's revelation and that the Church does not have a role of intermediary between the individual and God. Second, only the possession of the grace of God can bring one to salvation and the sacraments of the Church are not effective, with the exception of baptism and celebrating the Last Supper (communion). Third is the belief that religious affairs should be strictly separated from secular affairs. The religious faith of the individual is still above the power of the state, but as long as the secular activities of the state do not interfere with religious belief, the state is to be obeyed. Last, but not least, is the belief that the leaders of the Church do not stand in any higher relation to God than the individual member does. They are elected by the members and are answerable to the members for their behavior. The leaders are leaders in the sense of being guides to moral behavior, and the administrators of Church affairs. Like all Christians, the Protestants also accepted the basic beliefs that God is one, that he sent his son to earth in the form of a man, that the death of Christ on the cross redeemed man from the original sin of Adam, that the scriptures are the divine revealed word of God, that the grace of God alone can save man and not his good works, and that man is inherently evil.

The most important aspects of the period of time that include the Renaissance and Reformation can be found in the general movements they initiated. The Renaissance brought with it the tools that would later be needed to support the Enlightenment. These tools included a general attitude of the importance of a critical analysis of all authority and the scientific requirement that all knowledge must conform to experience, i.e., facts. The Reformation brought with it a widespread dissemination of knowledge through its extensive use of the printing press and the use of the vernacular (language actually spoken by people) of the various nation states. It also brought with it a concern for the development of the individual in all aspects of life through the use of human reason (the concept that each person was capable of interpreting the scriptures for himself or herself). This latter would be imperative to the development of the industrial revolution and the continuing development of the nation-state (nationalism).

The Enlightenment was more an extension of the preceding movements than an independent movement. It did, however, change completely the emphasis of the ideas that had formed earlier. The critical attitude that had been imported through the Islamic scholars during the Renaissance was now applied to all aspects of life and not just to the philosophical whims of the educated classes. The "higher" criticism was now applied not just to particular issues of theological debate but to religion as a whole. The result was a deep skepticism concerning the validity of all religious ideas. There had been skeptical individuals, even some skeptical societies, in the past but now there were a growing number of people in all classes that were not only skeptical but true atheists. They were capable of denying, and did deny, the existence of God and the supernatural in general and they submitted reasons for their belief that these did not exist.

The Reformation movement, in its attack on the Roman Catholic theology, had based its argument on the belief that the scriptures were the revealed word of God. This left them open to refutation, should it be proved that the scriptures were not the revealed word of God. During the Enlightenment the use of human reason (the higher criticism) was applied to the scriptures. The general conclusion was that the scriptures consisted of a large number of inconsistencies and outright error due to translation from language to language, and that they had been written down over many years, and in some cases centuries, after the events that they portrayed. In addition they contained many examples of superstition and magic that had obviously been taken directly from the preceding pagan peoples. In short, the final conclusion was that the scriptures had clearly been written by the hand of man for the specific purpose of solving the problem of social control and to settle the issues brought about by mankind's general ignorance at the time they had been written.

Thus began the battle between science and religion that still rages to this day. It can be definitely claimed as the first appearance of atheism as a real social force. It is usually seen as the separation of philosophy and theology into two separate schools of thought.

The period beginning roughly at the start of the 1600s and running to the beginning of the 1800s changed Europe completely in the areas of religion, politics, economics, science, and technology. At the end of this period, one can safely say that modern Western European civilization had taken the shape that it still has today.

In the case of religion, the arguments used by the Protestants against the Catholics were now turned against them and a period of religious wars began. Both the Roman Catholics and the Protestants were greatly weakened by the religious wars that continued until AD 1648. The style and venom of the arguments used by both sides, their inflexible belief that they alone had a hold on the truth, and the savagery of the wars drove a large number of people to question religion in general. This trend was begun by the Unitarians, who denied the divinity of Christ; they were followed by the deists, who associated God with an abstracted nature and denied both the divinity of Christ and the efficacy of organized religion. This in turn was supported by the growing discoveries of science that explained many of the natural phenomena that had always been attributed to God, such as the nature of comets. The battle shifted from a focus that centered on religious creeds to science as an authoritative source of knowledge.

The religious wars had also wrested secular power from religion and returned this power to the laity. It must be understood that the majority of the population of Europe, and its dependencies, were still very religious in their daily lives, even accepting without question much of the superstition and magic with which organized religion abounds. There was at no time a concerted effort by the educated and ruling classes to replace religion in the minds and hearts of the masses. Indeed, these classes even more clearly understood the role that they wished religion to play. They understood the role that religion had always played in the establishment of individual moral behavior, and the ethical social behavior needed by the government to maintain its control over the people. The ruling classes, as well as the educated classes, were now able to hold to their skepticism, or atheism, as the rules that governed their own lives, without interfering with the inculcation of obedience of the masses through religion. It is with this practice that the real effort at separation of church and state began. In the case of a few men, such as Descartes, religion was denied altogether and a call was put out for society to be based solely on the rules of human reason. This call was ignored by the ruling classes as impractical, but led to the concern of later philosophy, especially that of Hume and Locke, with government in general.

The same period saw the final consolidation of the nation-state system in Europe. Most of the modern nation-states had been formed by the end of this period, with the exception of modern Germany and Italy. The latter two delayed their consolidation for a period of some 100 years or so. The development of the nation-state, as we have seen earlier, was initially supported by the development of international trade and the establishment of trading empires. As part of the trading empire the nation-states also developed the colonial system and used their colonies as a source of raw materials. As the trading empires were slowly consolidated into the hands of a few states, the impetus of support for the growing nation-states shifted away from the establishment of colonies as sources of raw materials and developed into wars over the control of markets for industrial products.

Most of the states could not enter into the international trade system directly, as this was finally monopolized by England. Each area, however, did have specialized products that it was able to sell in return for profit and raw materials. The English controlled most of North America, India, and many places in Africa and the Far East. The Spanish controlled most of Central and South America, and some areas in the Far East. The French had control of most of North Africa and much of the trade with the Near East. Holland and Portugal still controlled specific areas but were quickly replaced in most areas by the English and French. In the states that led the way in colonial development, nationalism quickly replaced religion as the national faith. It also replaced religion as the justification for war, and the states now fought each other over control of colonies and trade. The major result of this was the stimulation that it provided for the development of ever more efficient tools for the conduct of trade, industrial and military production, and finance.

In the lands that accepted Catholicism, the old aristocracies had managed to hang onto most of their privileges by claiming the king's divine right to rule. This had resulted in a much more strict class system in these areas. This in turn led to restrictions on the development of technology and change in general. In the areas that had accepted Protestant theology, especially in England, the leveling spirit had increased the rights accorded to the middle classes in particular. This in turn released the technicians to a more free development of technology. The end result was the Industrial Revolution, which for 100 years or so was centered in England, and produced the advantages that allowed England to become the wealthiest and most powerful state in Europe.

The world we know, the world of Western European civilization, has combined all these elements into a system that has produced a society unprecedented in history for its wealth and concern for the freedom of the individual. Science and technology have been developed to a point where their influence is felt in every aspect of the daily lives of all us.

One result of the failure of the individual to understand the complexity and nature of this new society has been a resurgence in the popularity of religion worldwide. In many areas of the world, religion has never stopped playing a major role and even in highly developed societies, such as the United States religion can be called upon to manipulate people for political purposes. From this point of view it is evident that religion still plays an important role in the lives of most people. Part Two will concentrate on the continued development of these issues. It will outline the role that atheism may be able to play in beginning the process of bringing the battle between science (human reason) and religion to a conclusion.

Before heading into Part Two, it will be useful to return to the concept of methodology set forth in the Introduction. We have followed, in outline form, the development of mankind throughout history up until very recent times. We have seen that to a very large degree this evolution has been the story of mankind's social, political, economic and religious development. In relation to our methodology the story can also be seen as the ever increasing ability to reorganize the data received by the brain as raw material into more complex systems of thought.

With a few exceptions, this procedure has had the following effects on the concept of religion. Initially, religion consisted of a very diffuse system of thought, as far as we have been able to reconstruct man's earliest days — to be sure, mostly through conjecture based on limited direct evidence. There may have been some system in place in which man noticed that he dreamed of those who had died and he was unable to separate the dream from the reality of their having lived. It can be conjectured that he had a sense that there must be an afterlife. The only fact that support this supposition is that a few burials have been found that appear to have been intentional — at least, those who found them considered that they showed care and intent — and the fact that some of the bodies appear to have been painted. The conjecture that Neanderthal man had a concept of the afterlife is only one possible explanation for that. It is quite possible that the burials were accidental or done for some specific purpose now unknown to us. The bodies may have been painted while they were alive. Any number of plausible explanations can be drawn from such basic facts. We, therefore, can either accept or not accept the hypothesis that Neanderthal had a concept of the supernatural as it would be experienced in the form of an afterlife. It is unproven, but it is a reasonable explanation.

We can also see from the archeological record that Neanderthal had come some distance in his ability to reorganize the raw data of his senses into systems of thought. He was capable of making tools, many of which have been found. He was capable of determining that caves would protect him from the harsh winter weather of the European ice age. This may be enough to show that he had already begun to change the environment he lived in by remaking the materials of which it consisted into tools.

The arrival of modern man, as opposed to Neanderthal (who may or may not have been of the same species), we see an advance in ability to reorganize the basic data of the senses into a more complex system. Early modern man left a form of primitive record. The cave paintings found in France, and dated to the time period beginning some 28,000 years ago, tell us a story that has several different levels in relation to our methodology. First, the reorganization of the basic data had now gone from a simple conversion of the data to internal visual, and probably verbal, images to one that also included external visual images. Second, the experts in this area believe that the ability to paint represents a whole new range of organizational skills at the intellectual level. At the very least, it represents the expression of internal visual images into images that are public in nature. The paintings represent, at the very least, one individual's ability to "speak" with a public. The experts feel that it is unlikely that these paintings were done just for the sake of beauty or personal satisfaction, although this could in fact be true. The purpose for the paintings is truly unknown and we can only guess at what they meant to those who drew and saw them. We tend to assign a meaning to the paintings that fits into our picture — a meaning that would neatly fit with why we would have painted them. It is generally accepted that the paintings represent some type of ritual that is connected to the activities of the hunting of game animals. This is usually extended to the use of some type of primitive magic or superstition aimed at controlling the actions of the animals themselves. If this is the purpose behind the paintings, then it is again a clear indication that man had become capable of conceiving of ways to manipulate his environment. Indeed, it is difficult to explain why the painters would have chosen the most inaccessible portions of the cave to paint the images if the paintings did not have some special or secret meaning. Whatever the reason for the paintings, it has been interpreted as showing that early man had already conceived of the efficacy of using symbols to produce magic in some primitive form. If this is correct, then it is also true that man had conceived of a power that was greater than man himself. This would indicate that man had progressed from a rather diffuse belief in the afterlife to a specifically organized belief in the supernatural, which he could put to use for his own benefit.

The archeological record also gives us hints that man had also began to reorganize the data available to him into more complex social structures. For example, the finding of huge numbers of animal skeletons clustered at the bottom of cliffs has led to the conclusion that early man used some type of group hunting technique to herd these animals over the cliff. That is one reasonable explanation; it is also reasonable to think that one man could not have hunted the mammoth effectively and that this was, therefore, also a group effort. This type of effort would have involved the ability to communicate with several others at the same time and implies some type of leadership role for at least one individual. Thus, researchers have concluded that man was using speech, by this time, and had already began to use some form of division of labor. For our methodology it means that early man had already obtained the ability to reorganize the basic data of the senses into a complex system of thought which included the concept of controlling his own environment and also controlling the supernatural environment that he had created as an explanation of the inexplicable things in his environment.

The next stage of reorganization was based not only on the ability to reshape natural materials into forms that represented man's internal images but also to display his internal images to the public at large, not only verbally but in writing. It is fair to assume that mankind had been able to express his mental images in the form of speech for many centuries. The benefits of this skill, however, were necessarily limited by the number of people who were in a position to hear to the words expressed, and by the ability of the listening public to accurately remember what was said by the speaker. As we all know from the childhood game of whispering a sentence to one person and having that sentence whispered to a group of people, one at a time, speech is a very unreliable form of communication. Man's new ability to reorganize basic data had allowed him to translate speech into written symbols which represented the meanings of the words (or as a more sophisticated, more abstract development, to translate the sounds of the words into written symbols and then to read them back and retain the underlying meanings), was a major breakthrough for mankind. In essence, it allowed the comparison of one person's thoughts with those of another or of several others. It also allowed the record of this comparison to be preserved for future reference. It has also allowed us to go back and actually attempt to reconstruct the thought that was expressed in the writings. The period of time between the cave drawings and the appearance of written records was only some 20,000 years or so — a very short time when one considers that the evolution of man is believed to have already been going on for some 3 million years or so. It is possible that we have attributed abilities to early man that he did not have, or that we have attributed reasons to these actions which were not part of his intellectual motivation. He may have painted for no reason which we today could understand, and he may have hunted instinctively without giving it much thought. However, the rapid development of mankind's skills in manipulating the environment is pretty strong evidence that the theories presented by the experts in the field are correct.

As we have seen, this 20,000 year period had shown a great increase in man's ability to take the raw data offered by the environment and to reorganize it into complex systems of thought. Since the time of the first written records, some 8,500 years ago, it is hard to tell what abilities man has now that were not already available to these early cultures. They were capable of organizing themselves politically into very large groupings — cities in the case of Sumer and an empire in the case of the Egyptians. Economically they were able to administer a very complex systems of agriculture, trade, industry and fine art through the extension of the concept of division of labor. They had also reached a very high level of religious complexity. It was now possible, through writing, for a single individual, as well as a culture as a whole, to preserve and pass on a complete record of what they had been able to accomplish.

In our debate over the existence or nonexistence of the supernatural, the most important point concerning the written record is that each of the cultures expressed a different set of ideas concerning the supernatural. Different aspects of the environment were emphasized, depending upon the way in which that culture lived. A whole range of mythological story structures was created by each culture to emphasize what was most important to them. In short, each culture essentially had its own religion which expressed its ideas of how the supernatural was to be portrayed and understood. They also created different approaches as to how the supernatural was to be used to accomplish the goals of the society, and rules for interacting with the supernatural. Given the level of intellectual ability at this time, it is odd that religion has not explained why the "creator" had not shown itself, by that time, in the forms of revealed knowledge later claimed by our modern religions.

Instead, it appears that religion was the result of a gradual evolution of ideas concerning the supernatural, coupled with a growing level of organization that came to be controlled by one class of people. This seems to have been a natural result of the use of the concept of the division of labor. It also seems to have been a natural result of the power given to these individuals and the fact that they would develop a vested interest in keeping this power. Hence the development of the concept of the divine individual and the divine word. We have seen how all ancient societies used the development of religion to enhance the position of religion in the eyes of the members of the society and thereby use that position to control them in ways that had little to do with the supernatural per se.

It is at this point, probably as a result of the ability to write, that mankind advanced to the point of what we today call organized religion. At this stage, the system was based upon the "official" hierarchy of gods and goddesses, the specific rituals and mythology that surrounded them, and the divine nature of those who had been chosen to represent the divine on earth. We must suppose that at this point, and probably somewhat earlier in a less extensive form, those who were in control of contact with the supernatural could also order, or organize, this power into a complex system of control over those who were part of the society. This soon became a method of controlling not only the actions of those who believed, but also the believers' thoughts. The same rituals, magic, superstition that had been used for millennia to control the evil aspects of the supernatural were now being used to control individuals in a manner consistent with the wishes of those who ruled.

By the simple process of making the social order a part of the supernatural existence, rituals and procedures could be devised to create a desire in individuals to bend themselves to "community" goals. Hence the marriage of secular power (force) to that of the supernatural (what the leaders declared was "the good").

From this point, the story changes from the historical development of ideas representing the supernatural to one that shows the organization of these ideas into larger, more complex systems. Religion went from being an individual experience to being an experience shared by the whole community. If each individual could be persuaded to give up his individual good for the good of all within the community, the greatest amount of good could be obtained by all (of course, one can always question who is in a position to know what is "good" for everyone).

As we have seen, over the period of time that elapsed since the formation of the first true cities and empires, many different attempts have been made to create just such a system. Initially, a limited number of gods and goddesses from the large number available were included in the "official" pantheon, with one or a few of them being assigned prominence in relation to the others, as patrons of the community. Around this limited number of gods and goddesses, an "official" set of rituals and mythological explanations were assigned to explain how the individual was involved in the supernatural. In a short time, a limited number of mythological stories and specific rules were added to create, within the community, a desired set of actions and thoughts. These latter were the rules that were intended to create a uniform set of individual moral and social ethical thoughts and actions.

It was not a very long step from this level of organization to the development of what we today see in the religions of Christianity, Judaism and Islam. That is, a religion which is organized around the belief in a single supernatural being which is both omnipotent and omnipresent, who has communicated his desires directly to mankind through one process or another (such as prophets), the establishment of an "official" group of people who are assigned the task of interpreting the desires of this being, and the consolidation of these desires into a written form that is representative of the absolute truth about this being. We have seen just such a process through the development of the religions spoken of above.

In the case of atheism, on the other hand, the story is much more condensed. For most of the time period under consideration, atheism did not exist. The birth of atheism is usually assigned to the skepticism evidenced by the Greeks. In extant writings from their time, this skepticism is shown to have included a questioning of the supernatural in general, as well as a specific disbelief in the grosser forms of magic and superstition and the mythological stories that surrounded the Greek pantheon of gods and goddesses. Skepticism seems to have received full acknowledgment by the Greek upper classes but does not seem to have been developed into a widespread system of thought. In other words, it does not seem to have affected the society generally, but rather just one class of people.

Until very recent times, religion and the supernatural were able to hold the field without a viable contender. The basic attitude that supports atheism had been undergoing a steady evolution of its own during this period even though it was not expressed as atheism. Side by side with the reorganization of data concerning religious matters, man had also been slowly developing more complex reorganizations of the data received from the natural world around him. He was beginning to understand more and more about the natural operation of the natural phenomena, such as the sun, moon, wind, rain, and volcanoes. He also was coming to understand the thought processes he used in understanding these phenomena and had begun to develop these thoughts into a system that today we call the scientific method.

As a result, man was becoming more skilled at relying upon his own power of reasoning in understanding the world around him, and he began to remove some of the supernatural explanations for the same data. These beginnings, however, when compared to the importance of religion in the day-to-day life of most men and women, was minimal. Only within the last 600 or 700 years, have the systems our ancestors created become organized enough to cast doubt on the use of the supernatural as an explanation of the world generally. It was at this point that humanity had to develop an alternative to the supernatural explanation, and the alternative chosen was a reliance on experience (facts) and the conversion of this experience into systems of thought that were based solely on facts. This is the final point in the development of religion and atheism.

We have now concluded Part One, and a couple of general statements can be made concerning it. First, it has been shown that religion, as a fact in the experience of mankind, does exist, and that it has been a major factor in the development of human civilization. Second, it has been shown that the contents of the religious concept are based upon belief in a form of being that is beyond the ability of human reason to understand. Third, there is an alternative explanation for the existence of religion as a concept and as an organized system of thought, an explanation that does not require the belief in a supernatural being or the supernatural in general. Fourth, that alternative explanation has come to be known as atheism, and atheism is based upon the ability of man to understand his world solely through the use of human reason. Fifth, when religion is considered solely in the light of human reason, the principle upon which it is based is false.

Part Two will attempt to apply the concepts involved in atheism to the specific problems that faced the United States and show how they can be applied to effect a solution to these problems. In doing so, it will be necessary to contrast these solutions to those offered by religion over the period of its existence.

PART TWO

CHAPTER 6. A REDEFINITION OF ATHEISM

It is apparent from what has gone before that religion has been a part of mankind's evolution for so long that it has become almost a matter of instinct. On the other hand, the concepts that make up atheism are so recent in nature that one cannot wonder at the fact that atheism is still looked upon as some sort of mental aberration. These facts, however, do not in any way reflect the importance of the concepts included in atheism. It is true that atheism has never been fully developed as a positive social force, but has remained essentially a negative system of thought opposed to religion. In the following pages, we will discuss a view of how atheism can be developed as a positive social force, and a position capable of providing practical answers to the questions asked in the preceding chapter.

Going back to the common dictionary definition of atheism as one who denies or disbelieves in the existence of God, one can only say that that is a very superficial definition. It would be equivalent to saying that a Christian is one who believes in Christ. The statement is true, but it does not say anything of substance.

Before offering a more substantial definition of atheism, let's take a short look at the state of atheism in the United States. For some who profess to be atheist (and this may be the majority of those claiming atheism), it means nothing more than that: They do not believe in the existence of God. They have not really given any thought to what that means to them, and in many cases they continue to live their lives as if they did believe in God.

There are also those who not only profess to be atheist, but who have developed an argument to support their position. They can explain what it means to them to say they are atheists and they can support this claim with arguments. This is the position of most educated individuals who claim to be atheists but do not wish to enter the public debate in support of atheism.

Lastly, there are those who both profess to be atheists and have developed supporting arguments, and who are in addition willing to enter the public debate in support of their philosophy. In the United States, the atheist who is willing to enter the public debate finds himself taking a position against the doctrines of Christianity, to a large extent. Normally, you can find atheists taking positions on the opposite side of religion on important social issues, such as abortion, homosexuality, racial issues, women's rights, prayer in schools and the separation of church and state. All of these issues are clearly outside the scope of the dictionary definition.

The fact that the English language contains words (agnostic and agnosticism) specifically denoting those who believe that God is unknown or unknowable and that man can only know what is material in the universe, thereby rejecting totally the teachings of organized religion, points to the weakness of the dictionary definition of atheism. It also indicates that there are a number of people who have decided not to take a stand on the supernatural, but rather accept that if it exists it is unknowable. From the point of view of history, many of the philosophies that went under such names as skepticism, cynicism, stoicism and others have been labeled as atheist in nature even though they

148

professed a belief in the supernatural in some form. In the modern world, such philosophical positions as deism, rationalism and others have been classified as atheist in intent without evidencing a disbelief in the supernatural or even in God. This looseness in the use of the word "atheism" has led to much confusion as to what actually makes up the philosophical position of atheism. For this reason it is necessary to attempt to redefine the parameters for using the word atheism. Here, it is suggested that atheism be used when denoting those who deny the existence of the supernatural, in any form, and who further deny the existence of any type of absolute truth, or the validity of any authoritative creed whose truth is supposed to be accepted specifically because it is "authoritative." This would include the denial that the existence of the supernatural is unknowable, except in the sense that it does not exist at all. In place of the supernatural, and "authority," the atheist would place his or her reliance upon human reason. Therefore the definition of atheism would be one who denies the existence of the supernatural in all forms whether this belief is in the form of religion or absolute truth of any form; one who believes that first causes can, and will someday, be known.

As Western civilization has grown around the concepts of science and individual freedom, the war of words between atheism and religion has become less important as a social phenomenon. In many cases they are merely lumped together as opposite sides of the same argument and both are dismissed. It is true that atheism has failed to acquire much standing as a social force, since it has often relied ridicule and unsubstantiated thought to discredit those with opposing views. Atheism has become so closely attached to religion that if one discards religion, then one must also discard atheism. If atheism's only concern were the removal of religion from the minds of men and women, then success would also mean the end of the usefulness of atheism.

The fact that atheism, in today's society, sees itself as the opponent of religion is its greatest weakness. If it were correct to say that the evolution of religion over a vast period of time has made religion akin to instinct in most people's minds, then it would be folly to oppose it by directly attempting to refute that deep-seated belief. One only needs to look at the arguments of modern theologians to see that they clearly recognize this fact. The theologians have accepted (to varying degrees) the fact that the Bible is not an accurate historical representation of the life of Christ, or even a fair recital of the beliefs of Christ or the early Christians. They can easily dismiss this as the result of the writers' need to accommodate a less educated public. They can incorporate many of the theories of science into the body of their teachings, such as the theory of evolution, the theory of the big bang, and the theory of relativity by simply stating that we are now beginning to understand the methods that God used in creating the world. Ridiculing these beliefs or publicly ridiculing those who abuse the power of religion does nothing to combat the theology of religion. The theologians have even accepted the invalidity of the ancient "proofs" of God's existence, but claim that mankind's innate need for the supernatural is an inherent part of our natural structure. This latter position is what we mean in saying that religion has become essentially instinctive.

In the United States, the Christian faith is divided into two general methods of thinking. On the one hand are those who are called fundamentalists and who call for Christianity's return to the simple faith of the New Testament. They tend to interpret the Bible in a literal manner claiming that it is the word of God and that the word of God does not need to be interpreted. They call for a direct belief in the divinity of Christ, that he was sent to earth by God to redeem us from our sins by his death on the cross, and that all of the commandments of the gospels must be obeyed to the letter. On the other hand, the so called liberal thinkers within Christianity are more open to metaphorical views of the New Testament, less strictness in the imposition of the moral and ethical commandments of the gospels, and less reliance on a belief in heaven and hell and other such concepts. They both, however, base their faith on the divinity of Christ and his mission as the redeemer.

Other major religions have the same dichotomy of thought. The Islamic faith has its Shiite sect and Judaism has its Hasidic sect. Generally speaking, the two schools of thought are interchangeable with the modern terms of conservative and liberal, which are used more often on the political or social front. The conservative arm, the fundamentalists, are much more vocal and more likely to take a public stand on the issues that they feel affect them and their system of beliefs. They overtly and vocally seek to influence the whole society, and the politicians and the laws that shape the society. The liberal arm is less likely to take a stand publicly on the pressing issues of social concern. They are much more likely to work behind the scenes in an effort to exert their influence; they have also tended to concentrate on the indoctrination of the young through the parents, church and educational institutions controlled by the Church. They have been very effective in this approach. The training, of course, consists to a large degree in the inculcation of the basic tenets of Christian moral and ethical standards.

This difference may seem small but it is very important. The fundamentalist tends to take this type of stand on every issue he or she feels is important, seeing things as divinely instituted and valid for everyone, regardless of whether or not they contradict human reason.

The fundamentalist sects participate directly and actively in public debates about the issues that they find important. They publicly support candidates for political office that share their views. Through a broad array of media programs they also publicly show their support for various issues and propound their views on religion. A good example of the difference in the two approaches is seen in the issue of abortion. The Catholic Church, which is a member of the more liberal arm, does not believe in abortion. The Pope has come out with a forthright statement to that affect. The statement, however, is directed at members of the Catholic Church and only tangentially aimed at the general public. It is intended for Catholics and specifically intended to direct the actions of Catholics. The fundamentalists also are against abortion. Their intent, however, is not just to affect the actions of the members of their own faith, but to alter the actions of the general public. Thus, theirs tends to be a less flexible position than the Catholic one; in essence their position is seen as a divine law that is universally valid and must be applied without exception.

Atheists have taken two general approaches to the difference found in the two Christian responses. In the case of the Catholic Church in particular, and the liberal creed generally, the approach has been one of ridicule rather than substantive argument. After all, it is impossible to argue substantively against what a person believes. The most that can be done is to argue against the concepts that support the beliefs promoted by the liberal churches. In general, atheists take the approach of pointing out every abuse of religious trust that it can find concerning individuals who are members of the liberal church (such as the recent revelations of child abuse within the Catholic Church) and also in ridiculing the remnants of superstition that still remain in the ritual or theology of the Church. Little or no substantive argument is normally offered, no reason or rational position is offered that would refute the theology of the Church, or to point out how the doctrine of the Church allows the growth of the abuse that comes to light. The response to the fundamentalist position, although ridicule and non-substantive argument still play a part, is much more emotional. The issues themselves, when a public stand is taken, tend to create an atmosphere of conflict. For example, the current legal system of the United States reflects the fact that a large and vocal segment of the public has taken a stand that supports the creation of abortion clinics and the public awareness that abortion is a social as well as a religious issue; but the fundamentalist arm of Christianity has reacted very strongly against the general public's legal support of abortion clinics in their stand that abortion itself is in violation of God's law. They have publicly demonstrated against the clinics, even physically blocking access to the services provided. In some cases the emotions have risen to such a pitch that some people have bombed clinics and shot and killed doctors who provide the abortion services. The bombings are most likely not directly a part of the fundamentalist religious reaction against abortion, but the emotional nature of their public stand lends support to those who would, and do, kill others as part of their "pro-life" stand. This is to say that the emotionally-charged response of both the fundamentalist church, and the fringe pro-life groups, has created an atmosphere that induces actions for which neither group would be willing to take credit. The general public tends to reject both arguments as extreme, regardless of what may be each person's belief about abortion. The public, at least to the extent of its acceptance of the laws passed by the government, has indicated its support for abortion and will not change its position based upon extreme stands by either side of the issue. Atheism as a positive social force could enter the argument on the side of reason remaining neutral to both the vocal advocates of abortion and the even more vocal opponents of abortion. Atheism, by rejecting the absolute right of abortion in all cases as well as the absolute stand that abortion is a mortal sin, taken by the fundamentalist groups, could foster an attitude of compromise.

One does not need to look very deep to see the current condition of the two conflicting ideologies. The Christian religion, including both its liberal and conservative arms, continues to be a very powerful social force in the United States. Lately, that power may have even increased due to a growing church membership and attendance. The same phenomenon is evident in many other parts of the world. Atheism, on the other hand, has not established itself as a social power of any dimension. In fact, atheism may have less effect upon the public mind now than it did 200 years ago, even though there are arguably more individuals now than ever before professing to be atheists. The reason seems to be that religion, in all its forms, is not just a set of ideals that are more or less believed in, but rather is a way of life that affects the individual on many different levels. Religion has always supported, as part of its history, a very specific moral and ethical code. In short, religion has always taken an active approach in training and inculcating the individual to an unquestioned loyalty to the theology of the Church. In a very real sense the doctrines of the Church have also been constructed and applied in an overall way to accurately reflect the needs and concerns of mankind in the maintenance of social order.

Atheism, on the other hand, throughout its short history, has limited itself to a set of ideals that require no action on the part of the individual adherent. Atheism has been an either/or situation, that is, either you believe that God does not exist, or you believe that God does exist. Attempts have been made to establish so-called natural ethical systems, but these have not specifically been related to the concept of atheism. They have also set standards that may be worthy goals to strive toward but that are beyond the reach of the everyday individual (as will be discussed below). As long as atheism depends upon the use of ridicule and non-substantive argument as its most effective weapons, it will remain incapable of establishing itself as a positive social force.

CHAPTER 7. ATHEISM AS A POSITIVE SOCIAL FORCE

To become a positive social force, atheism must begin by clarifying the position that it takes in regard to both religion and the society generally. Religion, and in this country Christianity specifically, is still a viable social force. The basic tenets of religion are not subject to proof or disproof through the use of human reason. In relation to these basic tenets or beliefs, the most that can be done is to present the counter arguments that support the atheistic position and expect that, if the arguments are given a fair hearing, a thinking person will eventually have to reconsider and drop his or her faith in religion. The decision to believe or not believe remains with the individual.

What is the atheistic position as concerns the basic premises of religion? The atheist as a first step accepts the position that the supernatural does not exist. Therefore God, as an omnipotent, omnipresent being cannot and does not exist. In asserting that, the atheist must recognize that he or she is in exactly the same position as those who do believe. That is to say, the position is one of personal conviction; no actual proof can be produced. For the atheist to argue that God does not exist, that is, to seek to offer evidence proving God's nonexistence, would lead nowhere and is a exercise in futility. God does exist, at least in the mind of those who believe in the supernatural.

A more productive approach would be to offer the suggestion that an alternative explanation exists that does not require believing in the supernatural. This would include the presentation of possible alternative explanations for the development of the concepts of sin and of an after-life, and the creation of God as a supernatural being. That is to say, offering explanations for the tenets of religion that are based upon the development of mankind's natural intellectual facilities

Becoming familiar with the history of religion would be a fundamental part of beginning this process. Part One of this work is an attempt to present and analyze the history of religion in as concise a way as possible in accordance with the facts as known to human reason. Religion is essentially based upon two natural needs of mankind: the need to explain the functioning of natural phenomena that, in ancient times, could not be understood through the use of human reason, and the need to develop a system for cementing the creation of social units as humanity's predominant way of life. In this sense, the life of Christ can be seen as a fulfillment of the beliefs of the believers in Judaism (the coming of a Messiah), as Christ himself is reported to have believed, or it can be seen as an attempt to reform the beliefs of Judaism through the use of human reason, the ultimate failure to reform Judaism, and the later development of Christianity as a separate religion. The Bible can be seen as the word of God as delivered by his chosen instruments, that is, the prophets including Christ, or it can be seen as the natural evolution of one people's attempt to set up a reasonable method of cementing their social structure, either as Jews, or as Christians. The moral and ethical tenets of Christianity can be seen as the will of God in relation to mankind, or they can be seen as the natural development of those actions that lend the most support to any particular social structure, i.e., in this case the system that developed after the fall of the Roman Empire. As we have concluded, the results of the application of modern science and philosophy in the form of a higher criticism have tended to support the latter arguments. The still existing beliefs in magic, superstition, and cult worship are outside the concern of both organized religion and atheism. These can be best approached by the use of education and patience.

One example that can be used to clearly denote the difference in approach between religion and atheism is the concept of the "first cause." In the religious view, the first cause is seen to be God. Under the explanation offered by religion, at least the Christian religion, the creation process took six days. Within the six days God is said to have created all that has existed or will exist, in the form that it has actually taken. This creation included the so-called laws of nature, which from the beginning have determined the actual course taken by the appearance of all objects in the universe. The religious position as to the first cause is therefore very simple: the supernatural created the universe by some process that may or may not be knowable to mankind, but is given, in at least allegorical form in the Old Testament of the Bible. Science, at best, is merely a more detailed explanation of what God actually did in creating the universe. At a known point in history, the period of Greek development of the philosophy of materialism, the concept of God was replaced with an equally abstract concept of nature; under this philosophical approach, the world as it exists today is seen to be the result of natural processes, and is not dependent upon the will of a supernatural being or existence of any type. This alternative explanation was developed over time and in modern times starts with a natural process; the most commonly promoted theory is what is called the Big Bang theory. Under this theory, at some point in the very far distant past all that exists in the universe, or has existed in the universe, existed in the form of energy. For reasons not yet fully understood, this energy collection was disturbed from a state of equilibrium and began to expand. At the instant of release from equilibrium, the universe began to expand and combine, decay and recombine, forming new materials and different sorts of molecules which eventually developed into the universe as it exists today. The scientific community generally believes that this process is still going on, i.e., the universe is not static but is continuously developing. In this theory, the formation of the universe and all that it contains is the result of natural processes that can be known by the use of human reason, and scientists are bringing more and more insights into these phenomena every year. It is likely that, as the state of human knowledge expands, the details of this explanation will also change, but regardless of the details or the specific theory of how the universe began, the scientific explanation denies the need for a supernatural cause. It is equally unlikely that the religious explanation will change, regardless of the state of human knowledge, due to the absolute nature of the "truth" it sets forth.

The main difference between the two explanations is that the one offered by religion is seen as absolute, i.e., this explanation is taken on faith regardless of the detail that might be offered by science to show that it is not a valid explanation of what actually happened. It is not a matter of fact that can be tested against other facts, but rather a belief that requires unquestioning loyalty, regardless of, or especially, when it comes into conflict with human reason. The explanation offered by science, on the other hand, is not seen as a matter of absolute truth. It is offered as the best explanation of the facts as they exist at the moment, i.e., the theory which best agrees with the facts as they are known at this point in time. Science accepts without question that the theory of the big bang, as it stands today, is liable to alteration. When, and if, facts become known which show that the explanation no longer conforms to human reason, it will be amended, or rejected, and replaced with a theory that is in agreement with the new facts. The explanation offered by science is, so far, the one that works best in terms of conforming to facts as we know them and so, for atheists, this is the most persuasive explanation of how the world came into being. Since the explanation offered by religion consists of speculations that cannot be tested, it can be ignored

This removal of faith in some supernatural being, however, is not the only reason an atheist has for accepting the explanation of science. The explanation offered by science is based upon a method that best accords with human reason — it offers itself as the best that can be had under current conditions, but does not stand as a truth of any type. It also places the responsibility for reaction to it solely on the individual. It is the responsibility of the atheist (or any other individual whether religious or not) to study and to understand the fundamental differences between the two explanations. One (the scientific) is based upon natural processes that can be confirmed by test within the range of experience of mankind, i.e., by application of human reason, while the other (the religious) relies on the unknowable and untested suppositions of the supernatural, as dictated from beyond the ability of humans to understand in the use of reason. The religious position is based upon the concept of absolute truth, while the scientific position is based upon the relative state of human knowledge. Once the argument of natural causes has been submitted and supported with factual arguments, nothing more can be done; it is up to the individual to chose what he will or will not believe.

The issue of the first cause is important from the standpoint of establishing the ground rules for discussion of related issues, but in itself is of minor importance. It is important that the atheist support his or her denial of the existence of the supernatural with well-reasoned alternative explanations regardless of the issue involved. It is arguable that the issue of greatest importance to the atheist is how religion has been used historically as a tool to mold people's belief in the supernatural into a system that requires individual action to conform to only those actions that are favorable to itself.

It is obvious from personal observation, and the observations of recent history, that the supernatural explanation is still alive and well in today's society. It is also apparent from the historical record that this explanation was for millennia the only one available. While belief in the role of magic and superstition seems to be on the decline, most of us see (or make) little demonstrations of such belief from time to time: knocking on wood; avoiding walking under a ladder; making a joke to insist that it doesn't matter if a mirror breaks (we won't have seven years of bad luck) or a black cat crosses one's path, all point to the fact that superstition is still very deeply ingrained. In addition, one needs only to look at the modern practice of Voodoo (seen even in New York City and other U.S. cities with communities or ethnic groups that brought these beliefs with them) to see the existence of magical practices in the world of today.

If such primitive beliefs still exist, how can one wonder at the belief that still exists in the more reasonable aspects of the supernatural as developed by organized religion? The beliefs of modern organized religion, while not reasonable in themselves, at least have for support their concern for keeping the family intact long enough to raise the children, and to keep citizens' actions in line as a means of supporting social interaction, among other social goals and results. In short, the beliefs of organized religion in their role as the moral and ethical support of the secular system have had some beneficial effects. The system of reward and punishment, which plays such a large role in religious theology, at least has a valid social purpose i.e., the goal of making it necessary for individuals to act in accordance with a set of rules agreed upon by tradition to avoid eternal damnation. Today the main social support for religion comes from the belief that the moral and ethical codes established by religion (Christianity in the case of the United States) make this world a better place to live in regardless of whether or not the individual believes in religion per se. The argument of atheism is not that the Christian theology has had no role to play in building a viable society, but rather that religious theology is the result of human reason being applied to concrete problems. The crux of the argument is that human reason, as a natural process used by mankind as a tool to solve problems, especially social problems, used as one of these tools the power it found concentrated in religious belief. The addition of a supernatural element to this process seems to be unnecessary, since all questions and their answers are based upon the use of human understanding.

The atheistic argument would then proceed along the following lines: First, the existence of something supernatural is not necessary to explain the first cause of the universe. The theoretical structure of modern science offers an alternative explanation that is in agreement with the facts as known. Second, that the development of the concept of the supernatural, and religion in particular, has been carried forward by the implementation of rituals, ceremonies and theologies that are themselves created by the use of human reason. The theories offered by historians, scientists and others have explained the rise of religion, as we understand it today, in a fashion that accords well with the facts as we know them without the need for a supernatural will to direct them. Third, the beliefs incorporated in religion are based upon a truth which cannot be tested in any fashion. The theories of science upon which atheism depends for its support are testable against the facts of experience and can be altered to meet the changing state of human knowledge. Fourth, theology in religion, its moral and ethical systems, is based solely on the authority of the human beings that reportedly received them from God directly. The atheist bases his code of moral and ethical behavior on the needs and desires of mankind as established by the facts of experience and in accordance with human reason. It is the position of atheism that the arguments presented are more in accord with the demands of human reason and the needs and desires of the individual in today's society than are those of religion.

If those who wish to deny the validity of the above statements care to support their denial with arguments of fact, one can continue the debate. If the only arguments that can be submitted by religion are those which must be taken on faith, or the authority of men who no longer can be questioned, then no room exists for debate.

Many atheists hope that atheism will go farther than merely asserting that there is no supernatural, but that it will also offer a positive social alternative to religion in the field of moral and ethical behavior. The last two hundred years of experience would clearly indicate that the mere presentation of the facts that support atheistic concepts has no effect upon those who believe in religion. This would indicate that atheist, if they wish to see their concepts put into effect, must take additional steps. The adherents of science, both physical and social, have been unwilling to take responsibility for the moral and ethical consequences of their theories upon mankind. The exact sciences seem to have taken the position that they are only involved in explaining the actual operation of the universe and not with its moral and ethical consequences. The social scientists, while more concerned with moral and ethical behavior, seem also to have taken the position of merely explaining it rather than determining what might be the best route to a satisfactory moral and ethical behavior. Therefore, in our world the duty of determining what is or is not moral or ethical behavior has fallen back to the proponents of religion, by default. Although the secular governments have a large stake in the moral and ethical behavior of their citizens, they have also tended to take the position that it is outside of their functions to determine the personal behavior of their citizens, unless this behavior is in fact criminal. Organized religion has always accepted full responsibility for the indoctrination of individuals into its moral and ethical codes. Governments seem happy to allow them, or encourage them, to do it.

Before going into a specific examination of the role that atheism can play in the structure of the U.S. society, it will be helpful to fully outline the parameters of the religious position in relation to the U.S. specifically and contrast that with the position of atheism.

The United States throughout its history has been a very religion-conscious society. The religious orientation of this country has made it one of the most homogenous of any society that has existed. By and large, there has been only one religion which has held the forefront within this society. The U.S. has been solidly Christian in its religious belief from the very beginning. This religion, by law, has not been considered to be a state religion nor has it been promoted outright by the secular government to any great degree. The population, however, has been very largely Christian in its beliefs and the operative moral and ethical code has been that of the Christians. This does not mean, however, that there has been only one form of Christianity and in fact the United States is replete with varying beliefs within the general framework of Christianity. What has been seen in the U.S. is the attempt by Christians to incorporate the ideas of the Enlightenment into the framework of the older Christian traditions. This has led to a relaxation of the doctrines of predestination that held such a prominent place in the early Protestant creeds and its replacement with a creed which accepts that God will treat all people equally and that they all can be a part of the grace of salvation. It has also led to a weakening of the strict Protestant belief that man is inherently evil, that goods works and a moral life have no effect as to whether one will be granted grace or not, and that human reason has no part to play in the religious life. These tenets were all held, to a large degree, by the early settlers in this country who were for the most part Calvinists and Methodists.

Over a period of time, these doctrines have been replaced to a large degree by creeds which express the inherent goodness of mankind, the belief that both good works and a moral life will aid in obtaining salvation, and that each individual can use his or her reason to determine what is required of a Christian. As we have seen, this has led to the development of very liberal branches within the Christian faith as practiced in the United States. The Catholic Church is undoubtedly the most traditional and least liberal of the liberal arm, which also includes the Unitarians and other independent churches. It has also, especially in recent times, led to a counter-reaction — in response to the softening of Christian doctrine, a fundamentalist arm of the faith has grown stronger. As we have seen, this branch calls for a return to the harsher and more severe teachings of Calvin and Knox. This branch has been active throughout U.S. history but is very much in the public eye today.

The result of this trend within Christianity as practiced in the U.S. is that religion has for many people become again a personal experience rather than an abstract public demonstration. It is this aspect of modern Christianity that the fundamentalists feel to be the major failing of religion in this society. While they have also adopted the attitude that religion is an intensely personal experience, they also believe that this experience should be broadcast to everyone with the intention of bringing them into the "fold," that is, to make everyone else believe as they believe. The Christian Churches appear to have accepted the idea that God no longer reveals himself to man the way he did during Biblical times. They no longer expect public miracles to be performed by either God or the individuals who represent him in the Church, at least not publicly the way they did in times past. Instead, they believe in miracles but only those that are private to the individual or hidden from the direct view of others. God has offered salvation to all men and women through Christ and does not seem to be actively involved with the fate of mankind.

As was stated earlier, atheism cannot and should not attempt to argue directly with those who believe in religion as the only "truth" in understanding the world. That is what they believe and any attempt to prove that they do not believe it will be necessarily a failure. In the U.S., the tenets of the Enlightenment have found a home that can be rivaled by no other country. The concept of human reason as expressed by the scientific method and the growth of technological discovery has become a part of the life of every citizen of this country. A good share of our education is attuned to making us aware of the importance and great progress that has been made by the use of the scientific method. We share firsthand the benefits, and evils, of a technology that seems to have no bounds. It may even be fair to say that, at this time, more effort and time is expended by the individual student in learning and understanding the scientific method than is spent in learning the tenets of religion. This, of course, is not intended to mean that the tenets of the scientific method are more important to the student than the tenets of religion. There is room to believe, in fact, that religion has a larger place in the lives of most students than science has. What is important to our discussion is that nearly everyone in this society is capable of understanding what is meant by the statement that human reason is best exemplified by the scientific method. Most are also aware of the success of science in explaining the workings of the physical universe, and its successes in developing technology that makes man's life easier and arguably more comfortable.

Under the conditions set forth above, atheism would therefore approach the question of religion in this society in the following manner. In relation to the most basic religious belief, the belief that God exists as an omnipotent, omnipresent spiritual being, the atheist can offer the following argument. The only reason we have for believing in such a God is the testimony of people who claim that God has communicated with them. As must surely be clear to everyone, a totally nonmaterial spirit that is said to be incomprehensible to human reason cannot be known unless that spirit chooses to reveal itself. The only source of such a revelation currently known to man is the testimony found in the Bible or among certain men now living who say that God has revealed himself to them. In reply, the atheist can only answer that this source of information does not lend itself to being tested. There is no way to determine whether the ancient record, or the testimony of those now living, in fact represents a contact with a spirit of any type. If one does not accept on faith that the Biblical account, the teachings of the prophets, churches, and other sources is true, there is no grounds for believing that such a spirit exists. At this level, it is a matter of personal conviction and cannot be proven one way or the other. It is possible, however, as we have seen, for atheism to show that both the Biblical account and the tenets of the various churches have been derived from the constructs of the human mind in the answering of real problems faced by man, and that for this reason the Bible and Church doctrines cannot be relied upon as authoritative. Both the doctrines of the Christian churches and the Bible itself have been compiled from so many different sources over such a long period of time that it is absurd to claim that they represent the unchanging truth of divine revelation.

All the same, there are limits to what atheism can achieve in its arguments. It is possible for atheism to deny the story of Adam and Eve, the Flood (as an inexplicable event), the stories of heaven and hell, the story of Abraham, and all the rest of the Biblical account. It is equally possible for the atheist to deny the validity of the New Testament account of the life and teachings of Christ. What the atheist needs to keep in mind, however, is that these denials do not hold up to the standard of atheist belief any better than the believer's assertions do. That is to say, the atheist's denial is not based upon facts that can be tested, any more than the believer's affirmation of truth can be tested. The parties whose testimony is being challenged are no longer alive to check the accuracy of what they say or the accuracy of their sources. There are no physical facts that can be weighed against the experience of man. In a sense, the biggest failure of atheism comes when atheists attempt to argue against religious belief, at least at this level.

When we move away from the basics and concentrate on the specific tenets set forth by any particular religion, then the atheist is on firmer ground. Here, there is no question that these constructs are the work of real men interpreting what they say was the divine word of God. The theology of all religions has changed over time to resolve problems that arose among the believers. In many cases, what was interpreted one way at one time is now interpreted differently. What was once translated to mean one thing is now translated to mean another thing. What was once believed to be the eternal unchanging truth has now been adjusted, so that we have a new rendition of the unchanging and eternal truth. In these cases the atheist has available inconvertible facts in the form of writing, architecture, paintings and other sources to show that what is said actually is the case. It is in this area that atheism can play out its role as a positive social force. In this area it is possible to present arguments that can be proven to human reason. The tenets of the Church can be tested as to their compliance with the needs and desires of the community. A judgment can be made as to their continuing usefulness in the life of the society and they can be altered or rejected solely on this basis without any resort to belief in the supernatural. The rest of Part Two will focus on several specific issues that are now in the headlines of the American society and this method will be applied to them.

CHAPTER 8. ATHEISM IN THE U.S.

This chapter will consider only the United States. An attempt will be made to outline an alternative to a dependence on organized religion in establishing a moral and ethical standard.

We can start by recognizing that the acceptance of atheism has at least one ironic consequence. The acceptance of atheism clearly tends not only to destroy the belief in the supernatural, but also everything that is associated with the supernatural. That is to say, if one denies the existence or "truth" of all beliefs connected with the tenets of organized religion, then one will tend also to deny the "truth" of the contents of the moral and ethical code supported by organized religion. In this country, the main support for our current moral and ethical systems have come from the teachings of Christianity, so that if atheism is successful (in partnership with science and philosophy) in destroying belief in God and the representation of God in the form of Christianity, then it will also destroy the foundation of the moral and ethical codes now in force.

We also need to understand how the principles used by the founding fathers in establishing this country have affected the development of our moral and ethical codes. These principles do not necessarily have anything to do with atheism per se, but they do tend to strengthen the position of atheism in this regard. Many principles were involved in establishing this country. Some of the most important for our purposes are the concept of individual freedom, the concept of the equality of all persons before the law, the concept of republican government and the concept of separation of church and state. When we compare these concepts, as we understand them today and as they were understood by the founding fathers, we can see that a vast change has taken place.

The concept of individual freedom had a very limited meaning for the founding fathers; it was limited to the idea that all citizens have a right to participate in the government that rules them. Today, the concept of individual freedom has political ramifications but is not limited to politics, and includes a much more personal aspect. Now, individual freedom is associated with the right of the individual to do whatever he or she pleases, as long as he does not break a law established by society. In short, individual freedom has grown into a concept associated with an unlimited search and satisfaction of individual self interest.

The equality of all men before the law, too, was a concept that had a limited range of meaning for the founding fathers. It meant exactly what it said: equality of men by law. It did not include women, children, slaves or even non-citizens. In fact, the inequality of individuals in their daily lives was clearly recognized and accepted by the founding fathers. Today we find that the concept has been extended far beyond the original intent of the founding fathers and now even denies the real inequalities of talent, physical ability, etc. that exist in life and tends to create an artificial equality before the law.

The concept of a republican form of government had a very specific meaning also for the founding fathers; a republican form of government was one in which the representatives of the people, not the people, elected the rulers. It was assumed that the representatives of the people would be those most capable of making the decision of who should rule, that is, the educated and wealthy. Even at this level, the definition of citizen was very much restricted by the use of property requirements, residency requirements and others to establish eligibility.

Today, the United States is not considered to be a republic but rather a liberal democracy. It is believed that the people have a direct say in who will run this government and how it will operate on a day-to-day basis. It may be true today that the United States is operating neither as a republic nor a democracy but rather as an oligarchy controlled by the wealth and power of specific interest groups, both public and private. More will said about this later, but we must recognize that many extensive changes have occurred in the United States over the last 200 years. These changes must be taken into consideration when one submits arguments concerning a moral and ethical system for this country.

In the case of separation of church and state, it is equally apparent that the founding fathers had something different in mind than what we consider appropriate today. The founding fathers, in light of the environment in which they lived, saw the Church as a real danger in its influence over secular government. The recent history of their times had witnessed the struggle of the new national governments of Europe to free themselves from interference by the Catholic Church. The intention of the founding fathers went no further than establishing, in writing, the freedom to worship as one saw fit, and the principle that the Church was to have no have part in the operation of the government, and vice versa. The founding fathers saw government as an institution of man's own creation and not of divine inspiration. The government did not need the blessing of the Church. The founding fathers, however, did fully grant to religion its role as the teacher and enforcer of individual moral behavior, and through individual moral behavior, the establishment of a system of ethical social behavior. Their intention was to truly separate the functions of government and religion, limiting both to their respective fields of endeavor. This concept of separation of church and state has been upheld throughout U.S. history in a very stable fashion. It appears, however, that today the tendency is for the people to expect that the government will either take responsibility for the functions of the Church or guarantee that the Church performs its functions in the area of moral and ethical training.

Lastly, one must consider the fact that the United States over its history has become a nation ruled by law. The government has become responsible for the enacting, operation and enforcement of laws that now affect every aspect of the citizen's daily life. The Constitution is the original source of the law, but over time the legislative and judicial branches of government have become equally important as interpreters of the Constitution. Initially, the Constitution was seen as defining the specific areas in which the federal government was to be able to act and every other power was to be left to the states or the individual. Over time, however, the federal government has slowly expanded its power and has taken over many of the responsibilities that would have been given to the states by the Constitution. Individual rights, through the Bill of Rights, were included in the written portion of the Constitution. These rights have been greatly expanded by the use of judicial interpretation. It is unlikely, for example that the founding fathers would have extended the freedom of speech to include the right of gays to demonstrate in public. The rights of citizens have also been diminished in some areas through the passing of state or federal laws. For example, the Constitution contains the right of individuals to bear arms. This right has been restricted, and in some cases denied, by the laws of some states, and in the case of some weapons by the federal government. Therefore, although the Constitution itself has changed little over the last 200 years, the intentions that it represented have changed vastly under the doctrine of judicial review and legislative and executive prerogative.

As matters stand today, one hears a lot of discussion concerning the default of both organized religion and the secular government in the area of morality.

Such discussion normally revolves around such ideas as the dissolution of family values, the lack of respect for tradition, the lack of respect for the law and even a lack of respect for life itself. Many see the problem as a result of the absence of a realistic moral and ethical system upon which an individual can judge his or her actions. Some fear that the continued application of an antiquated, or non-existent, moral standard will result in the breakdown of society as we know it. They cite the growing rate of crime, the lack of credibility of both church and government in the minds of a large segment of the population, increased flight to drugs and alcohol as a means of escape, and the growing sense of skepticism generally in the young as examples of that breakdown. If these conclusions are true, to any degree, we must ask what can be done to halt this breakdown. Is a change necessary?

There is no doubt that mankind will continue to live in some type of organized society for the foreseeable future. Thus it behooves us to prevent the total breakdown of society in both the U.S. and the world generally. Whether or not the current situation in the U.S. represents the beginning of a breakdown of the society as it has existed for the last 200 years is still open to debate. If the growing rate of crime and lack of respect for the traditional supports of social structure are signs of breakdown, then human reason must be used to determine whether or not that process can be halted. If it is determined that they are merely a circumstance of modern life and do not threaten to do any permanent damage, then human reason still must be applied to alter them in a fashion which will eliminate the problems that arise from them.

Parents and the Church have, in the past, instilled this moral code in the individual and the code instilled was that of Protestant Christianity to a large degree. In the U.S. the slow incorporation of education into the public sphere has weakened the position of both the Church and parents in the performance of this duty. The public education system has shifted from teaching moral and ethical standards that was the mainstay of early American education, to merely teaching skills that will make the individual competitive in the world of work. The growing level of skepticism in each succeeding generation apparently has also weakened the effect of parents and Church in carrying out the duty of establishing a workable moral and ethical system based on the tenets of Christianity. The expanding role of work today — with both parents working, and the children either left on their own or placed in daycare facilities — has also lessened the opportunities for moral and ethical training within the family. If the Church, the school and the family are no longer in a position to be responsible for the teaching and enforcement of a workable moral and ethical code, then it seems reasonable to fear a social breakdown, or the lessening of dependence on traditional family values and the lack of respect for the law, government and life. These breakdowns in turn lead to an erosion of what can be called social levels of trust, i.e., the ability of individuals to believe that they will be treated justly by other individuals.Religion is at once the most important foundation history has offered for peaceful social cohabitation, and one of the easiest levers to activate in starting a war. This has been shown to be true not only among Christians, Jews, and Muslims but among adherents of Far Eastern religions or philosophies as well, including Hinduism, Shintoism and Buddhism. The various secular governments have neither been able to prevent the development of hatred among religious sects not to replace them with a positive social force. The governments have normally taken the approach that by enacting laws and enforcing them, they can overcome such hatreds and lack of respect for traditional systems of moral and ethical behavior. It is evident that this system has not worked well. The rule of law appears to have failed mainly because respect for the law, and obedience to it, have to be established before the law can be effective. This in turn requires that the individual have at hand a moral and ethical system that he believes to be in his best interest to follow.

History, as a guide to present action, strongly indicates that if nothing is done to reverse this process, then time will take care of the problem for us —

however, that may indeed entail the breakdown of society as we know it, and the reestablishment of society along lines beyond our control. This would include a great deal of suffering on the part of the individual and society generally. The alternative, of course, is to establish a system now that will either direct the breakdown, or provide a means whereby the new system created to replace it will be planned through human effort and reason. It will require a great deal of effort and thought to determine exactly what is wrong with the current system, if anything, and what principles can be established to correct the situation.

It is this author's opinion that one cannot do much better than to start with the concepts laid out by David Hume in his essay "Treatise On The Human Understanding." Although his language is somewhat archaic and his ideas are not totally applicable to today's world, his work is the best I have seen in the attempt to establish a social structure based solely on human reason. Hume sets forth several principles which he believes are the basis for all social structure (it is not the system that Hume attempts to set forth that interests us, but rather the concepts that he bases his system of thought upon). He asserts that the first cause for the establishment of society is based upon the self interest of each individual member of the society created. He suggests that the individual has a natural concern for his fellow creatures and that this sense of what he calls sympathy is the support that allows social structures to continue in existence once established. He further asserts that the learned behavior of mankind in society is based upon the obligation to fulfill the promises that the individual makes to others in the society. Lastly, he says that all other actions are determined to be either virtue or vice in accordance with whether they tend to support or degrade the social structure that is put in place. The latter includes the historical incorporation of the moral and ethical systems that are a part of the religious beliefs of the society in question. When any of these fails, historically, the result has been the breakdown of that society and its replacement with a new one. It is unlikely that those who found themselves setting up the first true social structures did so from any conscious understanding of their own interests, or any feeling of sympathy with the interests of others. The development of social structures, as we have seen, was a long term natural process of solving specific problems with specific solutions. The creation of moral and ethical standards of behavior was fashioned in the same manner, i.e., over long periods of time in response to specific problems that arose. What is of interest to us is the idea that it is the self-interest of the individual and the need to understand this interest as best served by social structures that is important to us. Hume offered many theoretical supports for his philosophy, some of which have been confirmed by later scientific research, at least in a very broad fashion. Others of Hume's supporting arguments are unsubstantiated or were disproved by later criticism. All of his concepts were based solely on human reason and that, for our purposes, is the most important point. The aim of his concepts was to establish a system that allowed the greatest number of people to obtain the greatest satisfaction of their self interest.

Applying to Hume's ideas the same methodology that will be applied to the problems within our society, we get a clearer picture of Hume's thinking. It was Hume's premise that mankind made a conscious decision at some point in history to band together in social groups. Hume's theory includes the belief that, at this point, all of the members of the group decided, by some unknown means, that it was in their self interest to work in concert rather than alone. Hume assumed that mankind had already learned by experience that very few of an individual's self interests were satisfied by sole reliance on his own power. Hume further postulates that it became plain that, by giving up some self interest voluntarily, with the expectation that others would do the same, conditions would be created that would allow them to work in concert for the greater good of all concerned. We , of course, do not believe in the actual social contract any more, but as an allegorical explanation of the effects of banding together in larger social structures it is fairly accurate.

Applying the actual facts of history, which were largely unknown in Hume's time, we can see that actually his theory does not correspond to the facts. Early societies, as near as we can tell, were not actually formed through the conscious efforts of their members, at least the majority of the members. Rather it seems that the earliest societies were formed over a very long period of time and were more or less the unconscious result of necessities that arose in obtaining the means of survival. If there was conscious intent, it would have involved only a small number of the members who had control of the force to make it happen. After the initial stage, it is more likely that social structures were created and maintained by force and the self interest of the ruling or military elite. Later, the establishment of their authority was legalized by calling it the will of God. We can, therefore, safely discard Hume's theory that there was a point in time in which men lived by the law of the jungle and decided consciously to make a contract between themselves to form a social group. History would also seem to indicate that the emotion of sympathy had little or nothing to do with the formation of social structures.

However, even accepting that the initial creation of larger social groupings was mainly unconscious or was determined by the use of force — and most certainly not by the use of human reason in open debate — one can still look at the history of social groupings from his point of view. It seems most likely that Hume understood that human social interaction was longstanding and absolutely essential to the continued use of social structures. Within this context one can postulate that the continue used of social groupings and their growing size and complexity points to the fact that they must have been valuable to the members of society in some way. It may have been nothing more, initially, than the protection of the strongest male or the ability to obtain more food, but value certainly played a part. We can therefore make a general theory that any social grouping will last only as long as it satisfies at least some of the self interests of at least the majority of the group.

Without going into any further consideration of Hume's ideas, we return to a consideration of the society represented by the United States. The foundation of the United States is the first known instance in which the conditions Hume described actually existed. That is to say, the United States did not exist prior to 1775 and the founding fathers who gathered to construct a society were quite consciously setting out to do it based solely on the use of their reason. The men who created the United States have a unique place in history and they knew it. All of them were highly educated; they were part of the intellectual Enlightenment movement that was remaking Europe. They were well read in history, government, economics, and knew how important were the changes wrought by the Renaissance and Reformation. Some of them, including Franklin, were also on the expanding edge of the growing interest in science and technology. Jefferson and Adams, two of the most broadly learned men of the time, did not attend the debate in person as they were away on overseas assignments; it is likely, however, that all attending the Convention were well aware of their positions on the issues. All of them had also been raised in the traditions of the Christian faith (mostly in the Puritan or Methodist traditions), in particular, the beliefs of the Calvinists. The point is that at the time of the Constitutional Convention, the founding fathers were keenly aware of the opportunity that faced them and were surrounded by a very homogenous environment (society). The circumstances could not have been better for the creation of a new form of social organization. The only groups not included in this homogenous grouping were the American Indians and the enslaved Africans. The Indians would not be included in the society in any way (in fact they were intentionally excluded) and the slaves only as numbers in the determination of tax and representation issues, in other words, the slaves were counted as an economic compromise to satisfy the states with a smaller population without being considered as potential citizens.

The very first official act of the United States was to declare its independence from the rule of England. The Declaration of Independence, drawn up by Thomas Jefferson, expresses three clear concepts: first, that the act was sanctioned and approved of by God; second, that the government of the colonies by England no longer served the self interest of the colonies and for that reason was dissolved; third, that the citizens of the colonies were free men capable of deciding their own self interest based upon the use of human reason. This instrument was set forth as the collective will of the individuals that made up the colonies — but probably it did not represent even the majority view within the 13 colonies. From the point of view of religion, what is important is the assertion that God had endowed men with certain inalienable rights, that God had granted the equal right of nations to exist, and that the protection of God was sought for the endeavor. From the point of view of atheism, the most important point is the dependence placed on human reason in the justification for dissolving the dependence on England. The document set forth the reasons that the colonists considered the most important to justify their actions and propounded the belief that human reason was the means by which the new nation should be created.

The next step was to actually create the United States after declaring freedom from England and assuring it by force of arms. After about two years of martial conflict, the founders were in a position to draft and refine what has come to be known as the Articles of Confederation. The fear of tyrannical government was still fresh in the minds of the writers, and therefore the Articles as drafted did not even provide the powers needed to insure the new government's survival. The government that operated under the Articles did have some success, such as the establishment of a land policy for the Northwest Territories (that remained in effect until the Pacific Ocean was reached). It is also of interest that the Articles of Confederation contain no reference to the supernatural and was drafted without the supernatural being taken into account. In the end, the Articles of Confederation had to be replaced by a government that had more effective powers.

The Articles of Confederation were replaced by the Constitution. The drafting of a new document forming a new government was an act which went beyond the power given the Constitutional Convention, but this issue was not of importance in the end. The Preamble to the Constitution sets forth in no uncertain terms the attitude of those who were to take part in drafting the Constitution: to establish a "more perfect union" by establishing justice, domestic tranquility, common defense and to promote the general welfare. The Constitution as written and accepted by the various States contains only one reference to the supernatural, or in this case specifically to religion. Article VI spells out the prohibition against using any type of religious test as a qualifying requirement for any office in the federal or state governments. The first ten amendments to the Constitution (which were ratified in 1791) also only have one reference to religion — the first amendment prohibits the federal government from establishing a religion or from passing laws that would prohibit the free worship of any religion (this is the basis of the concept of separation of Church and State). This prohibition applies specifically to the federal government and does not apply to the actions of the various states. If only the wording of the Constitution is considered, it becomes clear that the concept of separation of Church and State is more appropriately seen as a prohibition against the federal government interfering in the affairs of religion.

It is very clear from the foregoing that, whether or not the founding fathers intended to exclude religion from their work, they in fact did so. No amount of argument can change the fact that religion did not enter into the debate which led to the formation of the United States. It is not likely that religion was considered unimportant in the society being created, but rather that it was considered to have its own area of operation. Although the separation of church and state is not specifically mentioned in the Constitution, that was interpretation placed on the first amendment by the courts as the intention of the founding fathers. It is at this point that we see why Hume's discussion of self interest is relevant. The United States from its very foundation appears to be a perfect representative of a social organization that was created from the perceived self interest of the members which were to make it up. The subsequent history of the United States can be interpreted as the adjustments that have been made to maintain an accordance with that self interest.

It can also be reasonably argued that the lack of mention of religion in the Constitution was the result of the very large homogeneity that existed at the time, concerning religion. All of the founding fathers were religious men, as were most of the citizens of the new society. They were not only religious, but members of the same faith, even largely of the same sect of the same faith. One of the attitudes included in this faith was the belief that religion was to be separate from government and should only operate in its role as the indoctrinator of moral and ethical behavior. In this role, religion was totally in control of most education and social interaction. In short, there was no need to mention religion, as it was commonly believed that government and religion were to operate in two separate arenas.

Over the last two hundred years, the most pressing social issues that have faced the American society have taken a form that includes the dominant religious position in the United States, that is, Christianity. Atheism, therefore, when it attempts to face the issues by calling on human reason will necessarily also find itself faced with the beliefs of religion.

Chapter 9. Atheism as the Arbiter of Social Self Interest

When one looks at the United States today, it is not difficult to see the relevance of Hume's thought. The level of materialism is outstanding. (By materialism we mean the social concept and not the philosophical position of physical science.) Today the concept of materialism in its social implications is normally considered to be the accumulation of individual and public wealth and the priority given to acquiring the accoutrements of "the good life." When the concept of individual freedom is added to materialism, the result seems be a type of free for all. Each individual is responsible for obtaining whatever level of material wealth his or her talents can muster.

The political self interest of the individual, under this concept, is to a large degree ignored. As a consequence individuals, in the attempt to promote their own self interest, have been left to their own devices or have been forced to join with others into groups known as interest groups. The most powerful of these interest groups are the ones that have the greatest financing behind them. These include big corporations, religious organizations, and certain other large associations centered around topics like environmental protection, women's rights and gay rights. All these groups, with the possible exception of the corporations, present themselves as representatives of the personal self interests that make up the society at large. However, they tend to represent a relatively limited number of people, and their interests tend to be short term in nature. The long term interests of the society and the individuals who are underrepresented are seldom, if ever, consulted by the interest groups or by the government that is influenced by them — hence, the concept of the silent majority. Even religion, which one would think would represent the interests of all Christians, in fact only represents the limited number of Christians that are members of the various sects involved in the interest group.

In the case of the individual, one does not need to look very deep to see the effect of self interest as evidenced by the modern concept of materialism. The majority of people in this country spend the greatest part of their lives in the promotion of their employment, acquiring material goods (the good life), seeking entertainment, and education and other goals of a truly personal nature. Little or no time is spent in thinking about these actions in their relation to the society at large. Less time is available for promoting social issues such as family values, moral and ethical education and social skills.

According to Hume, the pursuit of self interest was the basis on which the social order was created in the first place. The founding fathers, in designing a new society, accepted the notion that all the members of society would gain, in the long run, by giving up some parts of their self interest since others would also have to give up some portions of their self interest in order to pursue common goals. This concept still operates today and is widely accepted. Therefore, any attempt to establish a natural ethic or to replace the ethic that exists today would need first to consult the self interest of the individuals who make up the society.

Atheism, as a philosophical system, seems to be in a very good position to develop this natural ethic. The goal of atheism is to promote the denial of the supernatural and any supposed effect it might have, in any form. This not only includes denying the existence of God and refuting the beliefs of organized religion, but also any abstract concepts that are promoted as the "absolute truth." This would apply to the theories of modern science when they are promoted as the only standard of truth. Atheism must be consistent in accepting the idea that all truth is relative. The relativity of truth to the state of human knowledge would also apply to the standards by which a society would view its code of moral and ethical behavior. What has traditionally been considered true for all men at all times would need to be rejected as a standard that is not capable of being instituted. The "truth" of any particular standard of behavior would remain effective only as long as it met the needs of the individual within any particular society, or at least a majority of the people who compose the society. The use of the scientific method, therefore, would be the best guide to determining whether or not any particular standard met these conditions; as we have seen the standard that is used by the scientific method is the agreement of theory with the experience of mankind as evidenced by facts that can be tested.

This current condition is not, however, necessarily in accordance with the self interest of our society. As with the theories of modern science, if it is determined that the currently accepted acts of killing are no longer in the self interest of society, then they should be eliminated or amended. The scientific method requires that the theories presented on a scientific basis remain in accord with the factual experience of human reason. If they do not, they are rejected or incorporated into a new theory that reflects reality better, that is, that matches up with what has been learned through experience. The same would be true of the moral and ethical standards that support social behavior — as long as they are in accordance with the experience of mankind, there would be no need to reject or alter them and vice versa. This method could be used to determine the factual situation as it exists in relation to the general range of self interest in the society at large. It could then be used to determine what method could be instituted to insure that the greatest number of people could obtain the largest number of these self interests. This method would also require that a system be created that would track the changes that inevitably occur in society and what changes needed to be made to the standards in effect. For example, instead of an absolute rule against killing, the scientific method would determine what facts, if any, exist within current social conditions that would allow for killing another human, and then establish the rules by which killing could be considered in the interest of society. The current Christian doctrine simple states that "you shall not kill," but as we all know, whether killing is right or wrong is now considered (at the government level, at least) to depend on the purpose of killing. One may kill in the act of war and not be socially culpable for the act; the state can kill a criminal, and so forth. In short, in the social structure of the United States there are socially acceptable acts that involve the killing of another human being even though the existing standard of moral and ethical behavior absolutely forbids killing. Human beings, by the use of reason, have determined that it is best to institute some exceptions to the absolute rule.

With this general frame of reference, one can attempt to develop a set of principles in the area of moral and ethical behavior that are in accord with today's lifestyle. Hume, in establishing the concept of self interest of the individual as the basis of all social organization, was simply recognizing a biological fact. No one can doubt the validity of the statement that each of us is most concerned with our own self interest. In a situation in which there are no controls over our personal behavior, people would do whatever they could to promote their own self interest above everyone else's. Social structures were instituted to settle this potential conflict; social control of some individual self interest would presumably make it easier to achieve other goals. That is, the society as a whole would be benefited by control of unbridled self interest by the imposition of a set of rules that defined acceptable and unacceptable means of obtaining individual self interest. These rules are what in every society, whether private or public, is known as the code of moral and ethical behavior.

Initially the only extension of our own self interest was in the interest of our nuclear families and those who could directly aid us in obtaining our self interest. Hume believed that these natural extensions of our self interest were possible because in actuality we saw them as the same as our own self interest. He also saw this as the basis of further extensions of our self interest, that is, extensions into larger arenas, such as the troop, tribe and proto-village. That is, he saw the extension of our self interest, and those of the nuclear family, as the same as the interest of the larger social group as a whole. It is this concept of Hume's that can be applied to the establishment of a set of rules by which the actions of individuals can be gauged against the overall needs of society. Only in the cases of great suffering or great joy are our self interests seen to be the same as those of mankind generally. The destruction of the World Trade Center towers on September 11, 2001 is a good example. The whole nation, at least a vast majority of the nation, felt what Hume called sympathy for the families of those who died, and their interests became essentially identical to our interest. This, however, is a rare occurrence and is not found to be active on a consistent basis.

We must accept, therefore, that even though our own self interest is our main concern, we are not capable of obtaining a very large degree of satisfaction when we depend solely on our own powers. History clearly shows that mankind has accepted the concept that the largest degree of satisfaction can be obtained by working together with others through social organization. It is the need to maintain social organizations that has led mankind to establish moral and ethical standards of behavior.

Most moral and ethical standards that exist today would not be necessary, or would never have even been thought of, had not mankind organized into social groupings. For social organizations to exist and operate on a day-to-day basis, they must have the support of the individuals that make up the organization. In order to have this support, the individual must feel that the maintenance of the social structure is in his or her best interest.

What type of behavior has experience taught us to accept as the basic standard that could serve to support our social structures? At the very least, justice has been established as one such basis. Justice operates at two levels, the personal level (which consists of the obligation to respect the duties imposed by a personal promise, as its most basic component), and the social level (which insures that we can expect others to also honor their promises). It is not in our self interest to act on our promises if we have no expectation that others will do the same.

Before going on to determine what behavior is required by the principle of justice, we should look at the system now in effect under the teachings of the Christian religion. One major pillar of Christian ethics is found in the Ten Commandments of the Old Testament. Four of the Ten Commandments must be rejected by atheism outright as unnecessary for the operation of secular society. They are the commandments that require us to have no other God than the God of Israel, the commandment to worship no idols, the commandment not to take God's name in vain and the commandment to honor the Sabbath. These all deal with the belief in the supernatural per se and have not been proven to be necessary for the creation and operation of social structures of any type, not even that of the nuclear family. Indeed, experience has shown that such beliefs tend to be detrimental to the operation of social structures in a peaceful, efficient manner. This is true even at the level of the nuclear family, which can be clearly seen in the resistance offered when children attempt inter-religious weddings. In addition, if we choose atheism as a positive social force to determine the fitness of concepts as the foundations for social organization, by definition these must be rejected. In the case of the commandment to honor the Sabbath, although it can be rejected on the basis of its connection with religious tenets, it may be one that would be considered on the basis of its intent. It appears that the intention behind the honoring of the Sabbath is that every person needs a rest from the pursuit of his or her daily activities. This has been recognized throughout history and days have been assigned for such rest in the form of holidays, vacations, sick days, personal days and other such methods.

The remaining six commandments are a rather simplistic attempt to establish a basic moral code for individuals to judge their behavior in their relations with others of the same society. Each of these cannot be rejected simply because they are a part of the religious beliefs of Christians, but must be analyzed to determine if they are in accord with human reason and are still applicable to modern life. These are the commandments to honor your mother and father, not to kill, not to commit adultery, not to steal, not to bear false witness (that is, not to lie), not to covet your neighbor's land, wife or house. All of these could find a way into a natural ethic if they met the standards established by human reason.

In addition to the Ten Commandments we can look at the standards established in the New Testament as part of the moral and ethical standards of the Christian faith. The basic ethic of the Christian Church was adopted from the concepts of Neo-Platonism, principally the golden rule which requires that each individual guide his personal behavior by the question of whether or not he would like to be on the receiving end of such behavior: "Do unto others as you would have them do unto you." This ethical rule, and others that were laid out by Christ, can also be seen as the basis of Christian ethics and morals. The early Church also recognized the fact that it existed within a larger society and that this fact required further duties. Christ succinctly put this forth in his admonition to render unto Caesar what belonged to Caesar. Christ also recognized the laws of society in his statement that he did not come to overturn the laws, but rather to fulfill them, and that his followers should obey the laws. It is accepted that Christ, and the early Christians, did not have an extensive code of ethics, since Christ made it clear that his followers should abide by the laws established in Judaism. In addition, Christ and the early Christians fully expected the existing order to come to an end within that generation, whereupon the kingdom of God would come to replace it. Christ, therefore, limited his teachings to what was expected of his followers during the short period preceding the kingdom of God. Once the Kingdom of Heaven had been established there would be no need of religious or secular law as all would be governed by the divine mind. After a time had passed and the Christian community no longer relied upon the quick establishment of the Kingdom of God, it became necessary to enter into more detail as to the standards of behavior expected of a Christian. Over the first three hundred years after the death of Christ, the Christian Church adopted many of the moral and ethical standards that were contained in the earlier Greek and Roman cultures (pagan standards of moral and ethical behavior, especially that of the stoics and epicureans). At first, the expected behavior revolved around the requirements necessary to obtain entry into the Kingdom of God: belief in God, belief that God, through Christ, had taken a human form and had come to earth, belief in the redemptive power of Christ and belief in the divinity of Christ. These were based solely on the teachings of Christ (as best they could be remembered), and the teachings of the New Testament gospels as they developed over time. The Roman Church quickly took the lead in establishing itself as the sole interpreter of the New Testament.

Later, when the Church also took control of the secular power of the state, it developed a detailed theology intended to control the behavior of Christians in relation to that secular power. This was accomplished over a period of some 700 years, first by the Roman Catholic Church and later by the Orthodox and Protestant Churches, as well as by the continued existence of the Roman Catholic Church. Over this period the Bible, both the Old and New Testaments, were interpreted to meet the needs of an ever-changing society. Without going into great detail concerning the various interpretations that have been offered, it can be said without question that the changes were made in response to the needs shown through the use of human reason.

As society changed in the expression of its needs, the Church has been forced to alter the requirements of its theology to meet these changes. Many of these changes have not stood up to the higher level of recent criticism as concerns their alleged basis in the gospels. This alone will not justify the rejection of the principles that are found in Christianity concerning moral and ethical behavior. Since they appear to have resulted from the requirements of human reason, they must be looked at from the point of view of their continued agreement with the needs of society outside of the claims that they represent the unchanging will of the supernatural.

The point can best be exemplified by returning to the six commandments of the Old Testament mentioned above, and analyzing them from the standpoint of their concurrence with human reason and the needs of today's social structure. We will look at one of them in detail and then give a short outline of how this procedure could be applied to the others. Let's start with the commandment to "Honor thy father and mother." Removing the religious contention that this commandment is the revelation of God, does it still accord with human reason? It may be that in modern society this commandment would mean something slightly different than it did when it was first created. The ancients essentially saw the family as a form of property in which the father, and sometimes the mother, had absolute control. This meaning has always been informally softened by the natural concern of parents for the welfare of their children. The ancients normally placed the responsibility for raising the child to the age of independent life on the parents alone. This included training the children to be responsible individuals and good citizens of the state. This duty consumed a very large share of the effort and assets of the parents. As a matter of justice, the ancients saw the duty to honor one's parents as repayment for the fulfilling of this promise by the parents and, possibly, a reminder to respect the opinions of those who are older and maybe wiser. This is a situation both similar and different from the one that exists today. The parents are still obligated by our society to raise the children to independence and it still takes a great deal of effort and investment. But parents today, while they are certainly expected to take a part in training their children, are not the sole source of this training. They may not even be the major source. It is also true that the parents are now expected to provide for their own future and not to depend upon the efforts of the children to support them when they are no longer capable of participating in society. The example of Sparta in the ancient Greek world shows that even the duty to raise the children does not necessarily fall upon the parents. Under the Spartan system the children were held in common and their training and raising was the responsibility of the state. In some societies (such as the Roman and Chinese societies), the honor due to one's parents was extended beyond the natural parents to include a long line of ancestors. The apparent motive behind this custom was the strengthening of family ties, which played a very large role in those societies. Obviously, there were many reasons why this commandment remained in force for such a long period of time.

The situation in the United States is somewhat different. Not too many people would accept as the basis of this commandment the concept of ancestor worship or its other religious connotations. The commandment is essentially a reciprocal contract. In short, the concept of parenthood and the duties of children are largely seen in a very practical light today. The parents are expected to provide the necessities of life, including the training and education needed to bring the child to a self-sufficient adulthood. In our society that normally means until the child has at least attained to a high school education. From a practical point of view it has essentially been extended until the child has obtained a university degree. Our society generally considers a parent to have been deficient in this respect if the child fails to obtain a self-sufficient adulthood. It is also expected in our society that a parent will "love" his or her child in addition to this concern for raising them to adulthood. The child in return is expected by our society to "love and respect" his parents and to help them, should they ever need it. Human reason, however, does not necessarily stand in agreement with either of these concepts. In particular, human reason would reject the idea that love and respect for ones parents is an absolute requirement of human nature. A public display of anything but love and respect for parents is likely to come across as dubious at best, and maybe "evil." Our experience in life, however, shows clearly that this is not true in all cases, and is subject to levels of intensity in all cases. Reducing this concept to the self interest of the parent and child, a different picture emerges. It does not take much thought to realize that the basis of the commandment is the biological necessity of the species. The parent, or someone or thing in place of the parent, must provide the necessities of the infant or it will die. The child, if it is allowed to live, is required to obtain these necessities by bending its self interest to those of the people or thing that provides them. This does not require that either the child or the parents feel anything even remotely similar to love, respect or honor. It does, however, take a great deal of effort, time, and investment to actually provide a child with the necessities of life for such a long period of time. It also takes a great deal of control on the part of the child to bend its self interest to others for such a long period of time, especially towards the end of the process. Psychologists point out that the famous period of rebellion that teens tend to experience may be based on the biological necessity of splitting from the parents when adulthood has been reached. As was the case of Sparta, there are alternative ways of approaching the problem created by the biological necessity. The parents in ancient Sparta apparently were in agreement with that method of raising and training children. The same system, however, if it were instituted in the United States, would meet with a great deal of resistance. However, human reason can find many explanations that accord with the way life is lived in the United States that make such a system desirable, i.e., the growing use of social welfare to provide the actual necessities of life, the growing importance of public versus private (parental) education and many others.

In our society, although the commandment is in full force, the actual responsibilities of the parents have been shifted, in some degree, to other organizations. The government in many cases provides the funds by which the necessities of life are obtained (welfare), as well as much of the training that the child receives (public education). The institution of day-care centers also provides a good share of the actual care that is given to the child on a day to day basis. However, this shifting of responsibility has caused a sense of guilt on the part of many parents who are forced to rely upon it, this guilt is seen to be the result of the failure to abide by the Christian code of morality and ethics still in place in this society. All in all, parents are expected, and expect themselves, to provide the means by which a child reaches a self-sufficient adulthood, regardless of the hardship this may cause the parent. Religion in its recognition of the biological necessity has added to it the further requirements of adherence to its other, related, moral and ethical tenets. We are all aware of the pressure applied by our parents, the public educational system and our peers to conform to the rules of this system. They are, however, clearly outside of what is actually required to bring a child to self-sufficient adulthood. The development of the concept of honor, and later romantic love, was used by religion to make it the self interest of both the parent and child to move in the direction the Church wished. Anyone who failed to operate within this system was threatened with eternal damnation, or at the very least, social castigation.

It is possible, therefore, that the Christian commandment to honor your mother and father can be rejected in relation to its connection with the unchanging laws of the supernatural. However, the biological necessity still remains, that is, some system will need to be set up for effectively raising children to adulthood and caring for the aged and incapacitated within society. We will look at what a more rational system might call for a little later.

We can now briefly look at the remaining five commandments and their position in respect of what human reason would indicate as necessary to the maintenance of our social structure. That one should not kill has already been treated above. but we can add that of all the commandments this one is the most amiable to human reason. Although even this is open to broad interpretation, most would agree that one is justified in killing what is necessary from the animal and plant world to survive. We also mostly agree that a person is justified in killing another if necessary to protect one's own life, that is, in self-defense. This can be extended to include the defense of one's immediate family and friends, as their interest is seen to be the same as our own. War may be justified as the killing of others who appear to be the enemy of one's own society. Human reason has, however, established situations in which killing is prohibited and has been able to do quite well with enacting laws to control that behavior without the need to rely on a supernatural prohibition.

These commandments are still very much in accordance with the demands of human reason. The act of adultery, and the lack of respect for the quiet enjoyment of material goods owned by another are contradictions of justice, which is necessary for any social organization. Therefore, in any natural ethic these types of actions must be included in the moral and ethical systems set up to control individual behavior. The concept of divine punishment for these acts can safely be dropped but it appears that human reason still requires that these acts be prohibited to protect the social organization. The same is true of the commandments against stealing and bearing false witness. They are, by the experience of human reason, necessary to maintain the trust that makes social organizations viable. More will be said on these matters later, but it is clear that all moral and ethical systems do not truly apply to the individual as an individual but rather to the individual as part of a social group. It can be reasonably accepted that the commandments prohibiting adultery, coveting another person's house, land or spouse, and stealing, all deal directly with a person's quiet enjoyment of his property. The ancients considered a wife to be a form of property, like a man's house and land. Our current view, reflected by the laws in the United States, suggest a different understanding. The wife is no longer considered to be property; the material goods owned by an individual are still protected in great detail by the secular laws but are no longer seen as a matter of divine sanction. The same, more or less, holds true in the case of adultery. It is arguable that for the majority of the people in this country, the act of adultery still carries with it the stigma of sin or divine retribution. It is still against the law in many states within the United States. The trend in this country, however, is to see a relaxing of the sanctions against it; it is more common now to see it as a natural consequence of the freedom of individuals to make choices. Adultery is more socially acceptable now than ever before in this country, but still carries with it the personal trauma of one person not fulfilling the promises made to the other. In other words, the commandments that deal with the quiet enjoyment of property, such as "you shall not covet your neighbor's house, land, or wife", can safely be rejected in relation to their supernatural sanction and left to the secular legal protection that appears to be adequate. In the case of adultery, it appears that the commandment prohibiting it is safely rejected as a absolute truth of the supernatural, but may have to be dealt with in its relationship to the level of individual promise. Even on this level, however, there is evidence that adultery may be acceptable to society as a risk encountered in everyday life and that it should merely be left to personal choice. We will again approach this later in relation to what human reason and experience might call for in relation to adultery.

The fact that man is a social animal is so obvious that it seems unnecessary to mention it. Every stage of history is characterized with one or another form of social organization. It can scarcely be imagined at what point mankind could have existed without at least the benefit of an extended natural family. It is even unlikely that the nuclear family ever existed as the sole form of social organization. If the chimpanzee is any guide to the evolution of mankind, the smallest social organization for early man would have been the troop. This type of social organization can reasonably be considered to have been instinctual. It is only at the stage at which mankind began to organize into tribes, proto-villages and other types of large social organizations that individual behavior began to be controlled in the interest of group self interest.

It is clear that all moral and ethical systems are the result of human reason being applied to the needs of maintaining a social structure. In light of this, a few conclusions can be drawn: first, that the content of the rules of behavior established are a direct result of the type of social structure under consideration; second, that the rules of behavior established in that social structure are directly the result of the environment and state of human knowledge that existed at the time of its creation; third, that as the environment, or the state of human knowledge, changed, the rules of behavior changed to reflect those changes. In short, moral and ethical systems of behavior are relative; there is no form that is true for all men at all times, i.e., they are processes subject to development over time rather than a static set of rules true for all mankind for all time.

CHAPTER 10. THE TASK OF ATHEISM

In a general sense the United States today operates under three concepts: the ethical and moral teachings of the Christian Church, the Enlightenment concept of the rule of law, and the concept of individual freedom and responsibility. Although in actual practice these three concepts have operated concurrently throughout the history of this country, there have been times in which they did not operate in agreement with each other. The three operating principles are a good point at which to begin in establishing a natural ethic suitable to modern life in the United States.

Christianity as practiced in the United States consists of a well organized and thought out system of moral behavior for the individual and ethical behavior for social interrelationships. In general, if one followed the rules completely, they would affect every aspect of the individual's life. Over time, some specific rules of behavior have been emphasized over others and have in essence become the basis of the whole system. One of the major areas of emphasis, if not the most emphasized, is the one known generally as family values. Christianity has placed a very high esteem upon the importance of the nuclear family. Some of the most important rules found in this area are the concept of monogamy, a bias against divorce, a bias against adultery, and the sanctity of procreation. These have led to public stands against divorce, adultery, abortion, homosexual activity and many others. Included within the concept of the nuclear family are a set of duties which include the duty to train children in the tenets of the Church, the duty to love your children and the duty to provide your children with education for future benefit to society in the work world. If one professes to be a Christian, it is expected that one will fulfill these duties in full. This would also include the duties to follow the dictates of the Ten Commandments and the demands of the Gospels. Generally speaking, the behavior that is expected of a Christian is in close accordance with what we call virtues and vices. The list is long indeed, but a short list will give an idea of what is meant. Some of the virtues that are of importance to the Christian creed are honesty, generosity, faithfulness, loyalty and courage. The vices would be the opposite, such as, dishonesty, greed, cowardice, infidelity, and disloyalty. Each of these must be analyzed to see whether or not they are, in fact, standards that can be met by human actions. That is to say, each of the virtues has both a religious and secular explanation, and use. In establishing a natural ethic each virtue must be considered as a possible goal that is necessary for the smooth running of society.

The rule of law, as it applies to the United States, is a quite different situation. The only, or at least the most basic, requirement of the rule of law is obedience. It is expected that once a law is put into force, all citizens will comply with it. A series of punishments is attached to each law for failure to comply. Some of these punishments are monetary fines, some are of the nature of social stigma, and others include the imposition of physical punishment. The rule of law in this country also includes a strict separation of Church and state. For this reason the state is generally prohibited from passing laws which are aimed at directly controlling the moral behavior of the individual, but over time this prohibition has eroded to some degree. It is, however, still generally true that when people think of moral or ethical behavior they think in terms of religion rather than secular law. The basic powers of the federal government are set forth in the Constitution. All matters not expressly granted to the federal government in the Constitution were intended by the founding fathers to be reserved to the various states. This intention has also been eroded to a large degree, through the use of the judicial review process and the passing of laws that usurp the power left to the state by the federal legislature. As a compromise, a Bill of Rights was added to the Constitution which expressly set forth what the founding fathers considered to be the most important aspects of individual freedom. The intention of putting these basic rights in written form in the Constitution was to guarantee that they would not be subject to encroachment by any governmental agency. The Bill of Rights was not specifically moral or ethical in intent, but it has been used in some cases to protect behavior that is moral or ethical in content when such behavior has exceeded the norms established within the Christian system. The Bill of Rights includes the freedom of speech, the right to bear arms and the right to assemble peacefully. Essentially, the rule of law includes not only the Constitution but also the statutes that have been passed by the various governmental agencies, executive orders and the body of common law brought from England. The latter is represented by a body of rulings that have been passed down by the various courts and are usually applicable only to the situation involved in the case under consideration. Since obedience was, and still is, the source of the government's authority, it has been strictly insisted upon. The idea of the law as the adjudicator of all behaviors acceptable to the society at large has tended to become authoritative in the same sense as the religious tenets of Christianity.

Actual compliance with the laws, as well as the control of moral and ethical behavior, was left to the individual under the concept of individual freedom and responsibility. There is no doubt that the founders, with the possible exception of Thomas Jefferson, envisioned that the Church (in this case the various Christian Churches) would continue to exercise a strong influence in the establishment of the desired behavior. This being the case, any of them could have produced a list of the types of actions that could be expected from the citizens at large. They would have included all of the virtues listed above and many others. In fact, these virtues have to a large extent dominated the individual and group behavior of the citizens of this country and still do to this day.

At the time of this country's founding, the vast majority of the citizens professed to be Christian and actively sought to comply with the tenets of the faith. These tenets were the basis of all education offered both by the parents and the school systems that existed at that time. The schools, when they existed, were directly controlled by the private interests of the citizens and were taught by people who evidenced a firm belief in Christianity. This training was normally supplemented by an introduction to writing, reading and math. This type of education remained in force until relatively recent times, especially in the rural areas of the country that contained the majority of the population. The whole of the education offered, both by the parents and the schools, was based upon the concept of a strong nuclear family and the consequent Christian values.

The last several decades have seen changes occur within the society that have put a very large strain on the traditional systems. There has been a large-scale migration of people from the rural areas to the urban centers, coupled with a shift from a largely agrarian society to one based upon industrial and service activities. In addition, there has been a large scale fractionalization of the society with the freeing of the slaves, and the immigration of large numbers of persons who held other cultural traits and religions. The education of children, under these changed circumstances, has shifted from an emphasis on the parents and Church to one that is dependent upon the public at large, specifically, to government-run institutions, i.e., the public school system.

The role of government at all levels has grown in response to the shift from small local communities to large urban conglomerations. Today, the actions of the federal government affect the daily lives of the citizens to an extent that almost equals that exercised by religion. The population has to a large degree remained Christian in its general religious beliefs but now contains very large segments that are non-Christian, i.e., Islamic, Buddhist, atheist, and many others.

Arguably the most important shift has been one from a dependence upon religious thought to a grounding in the scientific attitude. The growing specialization that has taken place within modern science has increased the demand for extensively trained individuals. Technology has developed rapidly in the sphere of consumer products, too, and now offers the citizens of this country a level of material prosperity that could not even be imagined a few years ago — although there are large segments of the population who are denied access to this material wealth for various reasons. The traditional systems that have operated within the United States have been slow to respond to these rapid changes. In some cases, there is a growing realization that the responses were either non-existent or totally inadequate, both by religion and by the secular governments.

If our analysis is correct, as the social structure has evolved the restrictions placed on the self interest of the individual have also grown, both in severity and number. Paraphrasing a comment made by Freud, the most salient aspect of modern civilization is the unhappiness that accompanies its growth. Freud believed that this general unhappiness was mainly the result of the conflict between self interest and the guilt felt when the individual is unable to comply with the ethical standards set by the society. He even indicated, but did not follow up on the idea, that the United States would be the best environment to study this concept. As an example he quoted the injunction to "love your neighbor as you love yourself." He flatly suggested that this command was in direct contradiction to both reason and psychological health, saying that this type of injunction was beyond the capability of most people to fulfill. In short, Freud believed that it was humanly impossible to love others as we love ourselves. Even more absurd, in his view, was the injunction to love your enemy, and for the same reasons. Any "natural" ethic would need to take into consideration this tendency to establish rules that the individual would find impossible of compliance.

Of the virtues and vices that have dominated the moral and ethical codes of the United States, many are either impossible to comply with or are contrary to human nature. It is, however, impossible to totally disband the existing moral and ethical systems, including the system of laws that are now in force — even though many laws also are impossible to enforce or are in contradiction to human reason. What may be possible, however, is to honestly assess the function of the systems in question and to remodel them on a basis that does not result in such a large degree of unhappiness. It should even be possible to eliminate the most unrealistic of the legal and ethical injunctions.

We must assume that both the nuclear family and the current system of government are going to remain in force for the foreseeable future. To establish a natural ethic also requires us to take into consideration the self interest of the individual and the self interest of the society at large. If Freud and Hume are correct in their assessment of the mainsprings of social life, then self interest can be seen as the very basic requirement of all attempts to set up a natural ethic. For the society at large, the self interest of the individuals who compose the society must be looked at in some fashion which allows the satisfaction of the greatest possible number of these self-interests. These two ends are not always in agreement. In the case of the individual, the satisfaction of self-interest would be the best when the satisfaction was immediate. For the society at large, the greatest amount of self-interests can be found largely in the restriction, or delayed satisfaction, of individual self-interests for the benefit of the society as a whole. In this difference lies the possibility of conflict, as it is not normally in the interest of the individual to defer immediate satisfaction of self-interest for satisfaction that is expected to be received in the future. There is no inherent difference between the satisfaction of individual self-interest and the satisfaction of the social self-interest of the society but the latter depends on training the individual to recognize that his or her greatest satisfaction of self-interest can only be obtained in social interaction. For example, an individual, or group of individuals, may determine that the greatest satisfaction of their individual self-interest involves removing themselves from any contact with the society at large. The society at large, on the other hand, may find that such action leads to a diminishing of the ability of the society at large to perform its functions and that it is in the interest of society to resist such withdrawal. This is in fact what happened when the Southern States decided to secede from the Union. The civil war was fought to preserve the perceived interest of the society as a whole in opposition to the interests of one region.

What does reason tell us about individual self interest? In relation to the prior analysis of the nuclear family, an analysis will be offered from the point of view of the self interest of the individual. It must be understood that the following is merely an analysis of the various individual self-interests that appear to be found in out society today, and not a blueprint for how things should be changed to meet these self-interests. It would be good if the following analysis sparked a debate concerning the points raised. It would be even better if this debate led to the establishment of a workable system that would solve the problems now faced by the nuclear family in the United States.

Biological necessity would dictate that the nuclear family consists of at least a mother, father and children. This biological necessity is recognized by the Christian Church as the only form of nuclear family acceptable to it. If a decision is made to restrict the nuclear family to only those groupings that contained this basic structure then it will also be in the self interest of the individual that some objective standard be set up to identify these members. Self interest would also dictate that the creation and operation of the nuclear family be solely within the choice of the individuals involved. In addition, it would be in the self interest of the family unit to have available at least the minimum amount of food, clothing and shelter to insure the continued existence of the family unit. A longer view of self interest would also include the idea that the family unit would be protected from destruction by other family units or the surrounding environment. We can designate this latter item of self interest as the quiet enjoyment of its potential of development as a unit. Within the unit itself, self interest would dictate that the relations between the members be in harmony with one another. Without these, the nuclear family would cease to exist, regardless of the intentions of the individuals involved. The status of the nuclear family in the United States is very much in agreement with the self-interests set forth above, in fact, the above description fits the historical situation specifically as it has existed in the United States. While this analysis is in accordance with the dictates of human reason as it is defined, is not the only definition under which the nuclear family can exist. As we have seen earlier, other combinations of individuals can be seen as representing the idea of a nuclear family.Regardless of the combinations of individuals that finally come to be accepted as the definition of the nuclear family, the consequences go far beyond the mere biological necessities in reproduction. At the very least, a serious consideration must be given to the biological fact that human children undergo a long period of dependency. The difficulty of maintaining the family unit during this relatively long period is obvious, and that is why each society needs to adopt an objective method of determining who will be responsible for raising the children. It is not within the self interest of any individual to be responsible for raising children that are not his or hers, either biologically or by choice. Under the traditional concept of the nuclear family, outlined above, it was not a problem to identify the mother or the children, but it is not always easy to be sure who is the father. And therein lies a great problem. This gave rise to all the rules against any behavior that could obscure the answer to that question, i.e., adultery, immodesty, and so on; and to rules that favor monogamy, to help keep the answer clear. They are, of course, set in motion by the difficulty in objectively determining who the father is, biologically, and the ethical requirement that the father be responsible for his children.

When one looks at the concept of the nuclear family in this way, it becomes apparent that the traditional system is extremely limited in its conceptual philosophy. There is no reason why the nuclear family should be defined solely by the biological parents and children. It could also include non-biological members standing in the place of the biological parents, or even the state standing in place of the biological parents. In some cases, this might better serve the self interest of the individuals who are involved, as well as the interest of the society at large. If the current concern with the breakdown of the traditional nuclear family, and the values associated with it, are accurate, then it is time that we attempted to redefine the nuclear family to bring it into closer accordance with the requirements of our society. Atheism, as a positive social force, should take the lead in redefining the nuclear family so that it will not be unnecessarily encumbered by the traditional value system supporting the current definition, that is, the traditional unchanging and inflexible Christian system. In this connection, it would be a mistake to limit the analysis of atheism to its traditional role as the opponent of religion. While many of the points that would be raised by atheism would contradict the position of religion, the concepts offered by atheism should be argued on their merits alone. Therefore, it is necessary to try and determine what the various combinations of individuals require in the area of defining the nuclear family and to change, if necessary, the definition to fit the current needs of society. For example, if it is true that a large number of people are making a choice, rather than being forced, into the single-parent family situation, then a careful look at the changes necessary to make one-parent nuclear families viable should be made by the society. Current research would indicate that one-parent families tend to be tied to the welfare culture and are directly involved in the growing rate of crime and drug abuse. Making one-parent nuclear families viable in our society would also entail addressing their contribution to these social problems, and possibly eliminating one factor in their growth.If, in fact, the father were not expected to take any part in the raising of the children, then these rules would make no sense. The traditional Christian concept with the nuclear family as its core belief requires the participation of both biological parents in the raising of the children. Under the doctrine of individual freedom, it is up to the parents to choose how they will raise the children. Their choices, though, are subject to the fact that society as a whole has an interest in seeing children raised adequately. The fact that mankind has always lived in social units larger than the nuclear family restricts the absolute right of the parents in raising their children. They are required, either by the application of social pressure, or by laws, made to conform their actions to raising the children in a manner acceptable to the society at large.

This method of analysis can be applied to any particular aspect of the current system of moral and/or ethical behavior. When one considers, for example, the continued existence of some form of social structure, the following concepts could be argued by atheism. First, and foremost, the concept of social organization can be seen as the result of the recognition of individual self interest. It has always been in the self interest of every individual to obtain enough food and shelter to insure survival. In addition it has always been in the self interest of the individual to secure protection from personal destruction. It did not take long for individuals to recognize that it was easier to take care of these needs by working together with others, sometimes many others, than to try to do it alone. It would, therefore, be evident without comment that it is in the self interest of the individual to be a member of the group most likely to obtain the ends in question.

With the group, relations of one member to another might be complicated and some system had to be devised to limit the actions of the individual to those that were of the greatest benefit to the group as a whole. The initial system used for this purpose, as is clearly shown by history, was religion. It was only over the last 400 years that the rule of law became as important as religion in obtaining this end. It was necessary, for example, to restrict the use of force among the members of the society. Religion set up a series of divinely-instituted requirements to accomplish this end: commandments against killing, lying, stealing and many others. The punishment for non-compliance with these rules was supreme: the guilty individual would be unable to obtain an eternal life of bliss. A supreme authority had to be claimed for these rules, in order to make them persuasive, so they were called "the will of God" who operated beyond the realm of human reason. The rule of law, although it did not base its tenets on divine sanction, maintained the system of punishments for non-compliance. In short, both systems were instituted to guarantee that the individual actions were in accord with the perceived benefit of the society as a whole. The net result in the United States is a mixture of religious and legal tenets into a system that has until recently been effective in controlling the individual behavior of citizens.

Are these traditional systems still capable of effectively maintaining that control? The growing concern of traditionally-minded people, that the systems are breaking down, is a sign that they are not capable of controlling the behavior of individuals. The individual virtues such as honesty, compassion, friendship and others all have their counterpart in social virtues — justice between the members of the society, loyalty to the social system in effect and a sympathy for the plight of our fellow citizens. The latter have often been associated with an identity of nationality, language, color and other non-essential factors. It is exactly these virtues that traditionally-minded people feel are breaking down. The growing rate of crime is attributed to the breakdown of individual honesty and compassion. The lack of respect for authority in any form is normally attributed to the breakdown of the virtues of loyalty and friendship. The social virtues have suffered the same fate, in the eyes of many segments of the population. These various breakdowns are all associated with the perceived breakdown of the nuclear family and its associated values as a root cause. Some of the most explosive of these issues are abortion, homosexuality, racial tensions and religious faith. The relatively larger acceptance on the part of society as a whole of actions traditionally rejected, such as adultery, divorce, public sexuality and others, also seems to be included. This acceptance is seen as a symptom of the breakdown of the traditional systems and, in all fairness, that seems to be an accurate reading of the situation.

Atheism, as a positive social force, as well as a personal system of rational thought, must find a solution to these conflicts if it is to play a significant role. Atheism can play this role because it is the least inhibited by the traditional system now in place. As stated before, in the case of the nuclear family atheism seems to be in a good position to create such a program. It has already been determined that if the traditional definition of the nuclear family no longer works, then a redefinition is needed. In addition, the above discussion would seem to indicate that a close look should be taken at the methods currently in place to insure the continued existence of our social structure.

In the case of the nuclear family, the problem as it currently exists stems from two different aspects of self interest. Obviously it is in the self interest of a growing number of individuals that the concept of the nuclear family be expanded to include non-traditional combinations of members. It is also seemingly in the self interest of society to find a solution to the problems that arise from reliance on the traditional definition — one-parent families, unwanted children and the difficulty of providing sufficient income and assets to raise the children successfully. On the other hand, we have the very strong bias of a large majority of people in the society for maintaining the traditional definition. Hence the sometimes very emotional debate that is associated with these issues.

The analysis that could be offered by atheism is based upon a long-term approach and would, of course, require considerable debate on each point. Atheism begins with the concept that the nuclear family is a fact of life, but not one that is divinely sanctioned, and therefore, outside our right to redefine as the demands of society dictate. Atheism accepts the position that there is nothing inherently against human reason in including within the definition of the nuclear family members that are not biologically included. The definition could include homosexual couples, persons who choose to have children and remain unmarried — provided they are profoundly committed to being a family and providing the stability and security over the long period of the children's development — and, of course, those who choose to maintain a traditional nuclear family. A definition that included all of these would recognize the changing complexion of our society and help solve many of the problems now evident, i.e., this definition would recognize the fact that a large number of homosexual couples are seeking to become parents, and that an equally large, or larger, number of people are choosing to be single parents. It is true that many types of homosexual couples appear to be unlikely to be capable of raising children, and that they evidence less concern about monogamy than traditional heterosexual couples. The current lifestyle of homosexuals, at least as far as becomes apparent to the public, would seem to indicate that they tend to be unstable couples, and therefore not capable of providing the long term stability needed to raise children.

However, this behavior may be the result of homosexuals being seen as deviant persons within the society as a whole, i.e., as social outcasts. It is at least possible that those who succeed in developing long term relationships, and whose intention is to be a family, will be capable of raising a child as well as many traditional couples do. It is also not necessarily true that single-parent families would be any less effective than those of the traditional type, as long as sufficient resources are available and the parent has enough time with the children to provide the necessary guidance and care. One-parent families headed by responsible adults can raise children well — especially is society helps out with a bit of economic support and by providing additional adult supervision including on-site child care facilities at the place of employment, and after-school programs. There is nothing "absolute," immutable or "God-given" in the definition of a family; some patterns are more likely to succeed than others, and adjustments can be made, rationally, to increase the chance of success for at least some of those who do not fit the traditional pattern.

If legislation were to be passed incorporating these concepts of the nuclear family, it would also be necessary to ease the restrictions on the adoption of unwanted children or children who become wards of the state through accident. It would also be necessary to reform the current system of aid to families to include families of the non-traditional type. Other laws, concerning divorce, property ownership, inheritance, insurance etc., would have to be altered to incorporate the realities of the new definition of the nuclear family. In addition, a system of education would need to be instituted to alter the resistance to such a program by those who hold to the traditional system regardless of its lack of accordance with human reason and the current needs of society. This would include an education that realistically portrays the lifestyle of homosexual couples, the realities of one-parent families and the need that all types of families now have for realistic social aid in the raising of children.

It would also require that atheists develop a well-financed and organized interest group to promote the goals of its philosophy. This lobbying organization could provide the avenue by which the legislature could be approached with ideas of reform or by which pressure could be applied to reject current or proposed laws that are unrealistic in relation to the general lifestyle of the country. By arriving at a realistic solution to the problems of the traditional definition, we would have the additional benefit of providing a curb on other social problems such as crime, drug addiction and lack of respect for persons, property and life itself that are so decried in our current society. The actual method of instituting these changes remains to be developed in detail, but the point is that an alternative attitude to the traditional concept of the nuclear family is possible. It is within the scope of human responsibility, not some divine outside force, to define it, and it seems to be in the self interest of both individuals and society to consider these changes.

In the area of social ethics, a somewhat different set of circumstances can be found. At least to some degree, the interest of the society as a whole contradicts the interest of the individual. Traditionally, however, social ethics has been seen to be dependent upon the establishment of personal morality. Atheism can fairly make the argument that this supposition is directly the result of the marriage of religion and government. If this is accurate (and history would tend to support the validity of this argument), then it should be possible to amend social ethics in a manner that rejects this attitude.

The government of the United States was formed with the idea that it could be operated without taking into consideration the existing religious sentiments. The truth of this statement is found in the written statement that there would be a prohibition against the establishment of any religion and a prohibition against any law that restricted the freedom to worship as one chose. In place of the sanctions established by religion, the founding fathers envisioned a system of laws that would depend only upon the obedience of the citizens as a matter of choice. Inherent in this conception was the expectation that law could regulate all relationships between members of the society on a strictly rational basis. As a general rule, history has shown that every society over the course of time tries to accurately reflect the interests of its citizens. When it fails to do so, it is either altered or destroyed. History also teaches us that every society, through whatever process, has tended to determine the majority opinion as to what constitutes the actual interest of society, and act upon that opinion.

Within any society of significant size, there exist an almost innumerable variety of lifestyles. Any attempt to reduce this variety of lifestyles to a basic set of rules applicable to everyone has been futile. If the examples that we have looked at indicate that the majority of people in this society require an alteration or rejection of the traditional values, that they find the existing definitions too rigid for them to fit into, then further attempts to enforce the rigid definitions will result in the breakdown of society, or at the very least will produce a short-lived, unstable, stagnant society. The 70-year attempt by Communism to accomplish just such a goal is a case in point.

Atheism, with human reason as its tool, should accept the fact that signs are showing a need to alter the ethical structure of our society. It should approach the solution of this problem from the long term point of view of education. It is likely that the solution will include principles that are contradictory to the interests of religion, but that is coincidental, it is not the main goal. The educational solutions offered by atheism should not be based on the religious issues but rather on the interests of society as a whole, updated to reflect contemporary needs.

The education recommended here would include, first, the point that the tenets which make up the current Christian value system, and the system that currently seems to be the major base for the existing social system, do not represent a unchanging eternally valid system of divine will. It is and should be altered whenever needed, if not rejected outright. Second, efforts to combat the notion that the Constitution and the law have any right to maintain themselves on their traditional authority alone. This education should make it clear that even the Constitution should be changed if it is out of step with the self interest of the society generally. It should also include the concept that such changes are a matter that requires much thought, research and confirmation as to their accordance with human reason.

It would appear that this is exactly how the system in this country was designed to operate, as to the law, but that public education has failed to instill in the public a clear awareness of the actual methods by which it is supposed to be accomplished. It is common knowledge that public education concerning the operation of the various levels of government is inadequate. As an example, we can take a look at the current situation with regard to homosexuality. The traditional system in this regard was the one established by the Christian Church. In the case of the most fundamental beliefs of the Christian faith, the only form of sexual activity that was acceptable was sex between heterosexual couples intending to reproduce. This sexual concept was even more limited by being acceptable only between two people who were married to each other by the ritual of the Church. By this standard, any form of sexual activity beyond what today is called "straight" sex would be viewed as a perversion. This standard still is in effect, at least from an official point of view. The general society, however, gives evidence of holding a different standard. It is apparent that a larger acceptance, at least from the point of view of social consciousness, has been given to many sexual practices that traditionally were considered to be taboo. One of the most obvious differences between the earlier days and now is the public display of homosexuality. Using today's terminology, homosexual activity has "come out of the closet" and is now openly public. It is also apparent that the open display of homosexuality has had its affect upon the traditional moral attitude. The result has been a general relaxing of the traditional moral standard to the point that in some segments of the society, it no longer exists. What has not yet been approached is the question of whether or not the new openness to homosexuality represents the majority opinion in this country. If it does, then we would be justified in calling for the rejection of the traditional standard — even though, as discussed earlier, those holding to the most conservative or fundamental view are often the loudest and most outspoken.

Each of the tenets of traditional social ethics should be viewed as subject to such an analysis, and when it becomes apparent that a problem exists, we should go ahead and conduct that analysis. The same method can also be applied to any particular secular law that is suspected of no longer representing the interest of society.

As an example, there is a debate in this country over areas that have been set aside as public land, and whether they should be opened to the exploration for oil. In the 1960s and 1970s, there was a very strong public conviction that such private use of public lands was counter to the interests of society as a whole. Laws were passed to incorporate this conviction into the social fabric. It appears that the current movement to open up the lands to exploitation has been suggested by limited interest groups (the oil companies) and it is argued that this movement is operating without consideration of the public interest. If it is determined that the public interest is best served by refusing the private use of public lands, then the laws restricting such use should not be changed; if, however, the public's interest is not best served by keeping the land "wild," then the laws should be changed to be in accordance with the current societal view of how public land should be used. The point is that the law should not be changed because one group pushes hard for the change; it has to be determined, first, whether adequate information has been gathered on which to make the determination of what is in the public's interest, and at a minimum the public at large has to be given a chance to voice its opinion through the vote, or some other method.

The last issue to be considered is that of individual rights within the context of the social structure. Initially, as we have seen, the founding fathers envisioned a system by which individual rights would be instituted by the direct election of those representatives most closely in accord with their own interests.

They believed that this system over time would involve the direct participation of a majority of citizens who wanted to participate. It appears from a historical perspective that this was basically valid while the society was small and compact. This has now become a practical impossibility due to the size of the country, the size of the population, and the limited number of people having enough leisure time and the funding needed to participate. The result, at least in this country, has been a lack of participation even in the process of voting. The actual members of a government are still elected by the members of their districts, but those who are actually elected tend to be members of the two major party organizations. These organizations tend to be operated by a very limited number of people within any particular district (the party organization). This seems to occur because it is the only effective way of producing a slate of candidates who are capable of presenting a relatively united front on the issues perceived to be of importance to the society as a whole. One result of the party system, however, seems to have been the trend towards solidifying party doctrine around a relatively inflexible political philosophy. Whether the laws, such as those affecting the use of public land, were the result of a true evaluation of public interest or the determination of a smaller interest group, they are subject to alteration or rejection only on the basis of a change in the law itself. Every issue that affects mankind should be resolved through the use of human reason. When any activity or belief contradicts the facts, as known to human reason, they ought to be changed or eliminated. The problem, of course, is how one determines the public interest, or at least, the majority interest of the society. The founding fathers believed that this interest could be determined by allowing all, or most citizens, to vote on the issue. Today the vote tends to be ignored by a large number of people, and the vote that is cast often is uninformed or based upon emotional rather than rational factors. Today it is fair to say that a large percentage of the laws passed both on the federal and state level are not presented to the public for a vote, or even for debate. The laws, for example, that control the use of public land were passed essentially because of the pressure exerted by various environmental interest groups. They may or may not have represented the interests of society as a whole. The current attempt to overthrow these laws also appears to be fueled by the pressure of a well organized and financed interest group who may or may not represent the interest of the society as a whole. This brings us to the last issue that will be discussed.

Once the "representatives" are elected, the "public interest" on any given issue tends to be formed by the well-organized and financed interest groups. This can be the interest group of a local district, such as a particular union, or of a national character, such as the National Rifle Association, or the combined interests of the oil companies, car manufacturers and others. No one will deny the importance of these groups in establishing an impression of what the dominant self interest of the society consists. They have been very effective in presenting their interest as the interest of the society as a whole. From the point of view of the interest group, they may believe that they represent the majority interest of society, or that those who oppose them are "misinformed" and would agree with their position if they understood the issue properly. In other cases, they clearly know that they do not represent the dominant interests of the society, nor even the wishes of the majority (right or wrong as they may be), but they know that they can influence legislation through their organizational and financial power regardless of the public's interest. On the other hand, interest groups do represent an effective method whereby like-minded individuals can make their interests known. This may, in fact, be the only effective way to make these individual interests known in a public manner. It is not the form of democracy that the founding fathers had in mind, but it may represent the only effective form of democracy applicable to very large societies. If this is true, then they must be encouraged to be even more active. At the same time, their activities must be made public and not be allowed to operate behind the scenes.

In addition, attention should be paid to how they are financed, and the open disclosure of finances should be required, just as (in theory) it is now required of the politicians themselves.

Therefore, for atheism to become a positive social force, it must accept a position that rejects its use of ridicule, crude jokes and unsubstantiated arguments in its attacks on religion. Second, atheism must replace these feeble tools with arguments that are substantiated by the use of scientific research, common sense, and the real interests of the social structure. Third, atheism must establish a well-organized and financed national interest group to act as the spokesman for the atheistic philosophy. Fourth, atheists, as individuals, must accept the responsibility of providing an education for young people that allows them a real opportunity to make a reasoned decision concerning the alternative to religion. This would include a commitment to insure that the public schools offer course material designed to objectively treat this issue. Fifth, atheists should make a wider use of the public media to promote the tenets of their philosophy. As atheism becomes a more widely recognized positive social force, through the institution of the means set forth above, the media should become more readily available.

On an individual level, Freud was onto something when he said that the unhappiness of social mankind comes from the fact that his self interest is repressed. Especially when a social system is founded on the claims of a supernatural system, they tend to require the repression of activities that are natural to being human. For this reason alone, we need to attempt to remove any remaining vestiges of belief in magic, superstition and myth that still control human behavior. Some activities may still need to be controlled, but only after they have been shown to be adverse to the self interest of the individual or the society in general.

219

Chapter 11. Atheism and Islam

Islam over the past few decades has become an increasingly important issue within the United States. It must first be stated that the concern over the issues raised by Islam are not religious per se. That is to say, the concern in the United States is not with the tenets of Islam so much as with the actions that have been taken in the name of Islamic belief.

Initially, our attention was drawn to Islam by the efforts of Islamic nations in the Near East to reverse the decision to establish the state of Israel. It is easy to understand that the Arab peoples, most of whom are Muslim, see the establishment of a Jewish state at their expense as a punishment for being one of the losing powers in World War II. The land on which Israel was founded was taken from them and they were dispossessed.

Secondly, the United States has become very attentive to the actions of several Islamic leaders which tend to involve what we perceive to be our national interests. It was our perception of our own self interest that brought us to support the Shah of Iran rather than any consideration of the self interest of the people of Iran. It is our perception of our self interest that continues our support for Israel regardless of the self interest of the peoples of Palestine or Israel. In general, the issues raised concerning our perceived self interest have consistently put the United States in an anti-Islamic position. This is true even if we discard the idea of religion totally and only look at the positions we have taken from the vantage point of reason. It is only natural that the Islamic world should react to this position by adopting a position that is essentially anti-American.

This general picture has now existed for several decades and has been justified by the government of the United States without any condemnation of Islam as a religion. Even in the case of Israel, our position has carefully avoided justification along religious lines and has centered on our role as peacemaker in the area. It is, of course, in our self interest to maintain peace in the area to insure a smooth delivery of oil to this country, to prevent the waste of assets in fighting a war, and for many other reasons. There is, however, clearly a battle going on between the believers in two different religions for control of the area of land now occupied by Israel. Both sides to this issue clearly see the conflict in religious as well as political and economic terms.

The issue raised by the invasion of Kuwait by Iraq was also one that involved our self interest in the oil supply. In this case, one Islamic state invaded another. The dispute was over which one of them was truly entitled to the land — at least, that was the justification given publicly by the government of Iraq. The United States chose to see the invasion as a direct threat to our national security and the security of all free nations — at least, that was the justification given publicly by the government of the United States. The world's governments sided with the United States and condemned the invasion, ordering Iraq to withdraw. The result was the "police action" known as the Gulf War. The Islamic world, at least to some degree, saw it as an invasion into their internal affairs. Whatever the case, it was again a position that put the United States in an anti-Islamic stance.

Until the attack on the World Trade Center in 2001, the issues raised by the actions of Islamic nations, and Islamic leaders, remained rather remote from the daily lives of Americans. There were human rights issues, there were protests against the actions of some of the Islamic leaders who were perceived as tyrants, and there was general support for our stance concerning Israel, but none of these were day-to-day concerns of the average American. The attack on the trade center changed all that, at least for the time being. The issue of Islam has now become a personal issue for the people of the United States. It is the response to this event, however, that atheism must focus upon.

Once again, the response of the U.S. government has been shifted from one directly involving religion to an issue defined as terrorism, from whatever source. In short, the people responsible, or at least those claiming responsibility for the attack, are Islamic in faith and claim that they were acting in their role as Muslims. The government has taken the specific facts of who is responsible and generalized or abstracted them to include anyone who might commit an act of war against the United States.

One very important point concerning Islam must be made before we look at the specific response of the United States to the attack. Within Islam, there is a tradition that allows a great deal of dissent from the traditional point of view. This has allowed Islam to incorporate many dissident ideas into its general structure. Within this tradition, however, is the idea that if dissent removes the party holding the dissenting idea from the general community, he will be treated as a non-Muslim. The general condemnation of the attack on the trade center, by Muslims as well as by others, indicates that these actions have placed the perpetrators outside the general community of Islam.

The response of the United States government raises two very important issues from the point of view of atheism as a positive social force. The government's stated goal of exterminating all terrorists wherever found, and of attacking if necessary any government which aids or offers safe haven to terrorists, raise serious questions. This approach has led to talk of deposing the leader of Iraq and the designation of several states as targets of our wrath, such as Somalia, Yemen, and Syria, and the Palestinian Liberation Organization. It would also include the destruction of the so-called cells of the responsible sect of Islam that we are told may exist in some fifty countries around the world. Resistance to this approach initially came only from the countries that had the greatest fear that the United States was preparing to attack them, but recently many more nations have expressed their concern and non-agreement with the approach. The disagreement seems to stem from attaching the war against non-state aligned groups, such as Al Qaeda, to legitimate states, such as Iraq. In other words, world opinion seems to be in favor of combating terrorism, even if it includes the use of force, but does not favor the invasion of legitimate states, even if they support terrorist organizations.

Secondly, the approach chosen by the U.S. government has included some temporary, and some permanent, suspensions of the civil liberties of the citizens of the United States. This has included plans to allow much wider powers of wiring tapping, and extending the power of the government to access private records, such as banking records — in some cases without a warrant, without even notifying the party under investigation. It has been stated that these additional powers are intended only to be used to search for terrorists, but concern has been raised that they might find other uses. The new legislation and laws that have been introduced, and in the case of the Patriot Act passed, under the general cover of a war against terrorism, essentially in practice would amount to a war against everyone, including U.S. citizens, as long as a claim can be made that they are suspected of terrorist activities, or the support of terrorist organizations.

Terrorism should be against the law, certainly; but breaking this law should be subjected to the same safeguards as any criminal act. The approach suggested by the U.S. government may be justified in cases where terrorism is seen as the crime of treason rather than a civil crime, but even this would not justify the suspension of the whole nation's civil rights. Did the government overlook the ramifications of its requested suspension of civil rights? In the specific case of the trade center, there is no denying the fact that those who claim to have organized the attack are Muslims and were acting in what they thought to be the interest of Islam. However, the question still remains as to whether or not the suspension of civil rights is a valid response even to this horrendous event.

Without going into any further specifics of the response initiated by the government of the United States, it is possible to outline how atheism would respond in its role of a positive social force. First, atheism would be forced to point out the facts of history as they are now known. These facts, seen from the point of view of reason, clearly show that every attempt of this sort in the past has been a complete failure. We can start with the general European response to the initial takeover of the Near East by the forces of Islam. The crusades were the response chosen by Europe and consisted of a military effort to eliminate Islam from the Holy Land. The effort not only failed but ended up strengthening the forces of Islam to the point that the traditional bulwark represented by the Byzantine Empire fell to Islam, as well as most of the Balkan states of southeastern Europe.

We can next look at the response of the Catholic Church to the heresies of the Protestant Reformation. The response was the Inquisition, which attempted to physically exterminate identified heretics and to cause any who remained undiscovered to repent of their beliefs. Again, this approach not only failed but strengthened the heresies to the point that they became totally divorced from the Catholic beliefs. Lastly, we can look at the persecution of Judaism, culminating in the attempt by Nazi Germany to exterminate Jews in Europe. The approach not only failed, it led to the formation of the state of Israel and an outpouring of support, financial and otherwise, that have immeasurably strengthened Judaism worldwide.

It is evident from these incidents (and many more could be found), that attempts to respond to a situation by exterminating either the idea or the people involved generally backfire. Not only will the response initiated by the U.S. fail to exterminate terrorists, it will in the end lead to the strengthening of terrorists, not only in numbers but in their ability to wreak destruction. Atheism, based upon these facts and their reasonable extension to the case at hand, would call for an immediate and thorough re-thinking of the U.S. response. Atheism would not deny our right to protect ourselves from attack by others, but would insist that a valid and reasoned response be chosen to effect this goal.

Atheism would also be forced to question any attempt to suspend, even on a temporary basis, any of the civil rights which are in force currently for the citizens of the United States. This would include, but not be limited to, the proposals made by the government to extend the use of wire taps, access to private records (especially bank records), the setting up of military tribunals to try those charged with terrorism, and any other action which evades the due process of law in this country. History clearly points out that any right given up by the people is very difficult to get back, regardless of the type of government involved or the temporary nature of the reason why the right was given up.

In this case, at least, there have been many voices raised in concern about these proposals. The concerns have in general not been against the use of the actions in relation to the problem of terrorism, but rather about the possible future uses that these powers would have. It must also be pointed out that the initial concerns about these proposals have died down considerably, leaving the average American uninformed concerning the government's current position on these issues. Atheism would again call for a through assessment of these issues and the release of the findings to the public for debate. We can expect no one to protect our civil rights if we are unwilling to protect them ourselves.

If the current military response, coupled with the suspension of civil rights, is not capable of bringing success, then what type of response can atheism suggest? If our suggestion that Islam is essentially self-correcting when it comes to actions and ideals that are considered outside the community, then it is our duty to follow up on the universal condemnation of the attack on the trade center. There is no question that those who join and adhere to this sect of Islam believe that they are acting in accordance with the laws of Islam. There is also no question that they would change their conduct if they were convinced that they were joining a group guilty of apostasy, thus removing themselves from the Islamic community. Changing the message that these people hear would take time, but would accomplish the goal of eliminating the sect entirely.

In addition, efforts can be made to limit the financing and arming of this group. The details of how the supply of finances and arms can be interrupted are admittedly difficult to determine and are outside the scope of our discussion, but at least some impact can be made. In fact, the cooperation that has been forthcoming from many of the Islamic states would indicate that they agree with this approach. The cooperation of the non-Islamic states in tracking down terrorist cells within their countries and eliminating them also tends to show that world opinion generally supports this approach.

Lastly, the United States should continue to seek ways to increase the level of internal security against such attacks, but only in a way that does weaken existing civil rights. Some of the increased security measures proposed and partially instituted along our borders, in our postal system, at airports, highways, office buildings and other public places are an inconvenience to citizens without necessarily infringing on their civil rights; other measures provide no apparent increase in security but serve to curtail travel and communication, limiting personal activity and hurting business and the economy.

The worst thing that could happen from the point of view of atheism — and reason, generally — is to forget what has happened and allow the approach chosen by Washington to run its course. Yet this is what appears to be happening. The cost, again learning from the lessons of history, will be many times greater than the cost of the destruction at the Trade Center, in both lives and property lost and in the quality of life and culture.

ADDITIONAL READINGS FOR EACH CHAPTER

Introduction

Poser, Michael I, editor. *Foundations of Cognitive Science*, A Bradford Book, The M.I.T. Press, Cambridge, Massachusetts; London, England, 1989

Hofstadter, Douglas R. *Godel, Escher, Bach: An Eternal Golden Braid*, Vintage Books, a Division of Random House, Inc.; New York, 1989

Hofstadter, Douglas R. *Metamagical Themas: Questing for the Essence of Mind and Pattern*, Basic Books, Inc. Publishers; New York, 1985

The Origin Of Religion

The Cambridge Ancient History, Vol. II Part I, edited by I.E.S. Edwards, C.J. Gad, N.G.L. Hammond, Cambridge at the University Press, 1970

Hawkes, Jacquetta and Leonard Woolley, Sir. *Prehistory and the Beginnings of Civilization*, Harper & Row, Publishers; New York and Evanston, 1963

Phillips, E.D. *The Royal Hordes: Nomad Peoples of the Steppes*, McGraw-Hill, Book Co.; New York, 1965

Rensch, Bernhard. *Biophilosophy*, Translated by C.A.M. Sym, Columbia University Press; New York, 1971

The Early Written Records

Kramer, Samuel Noah. From the Tablets of Sumer, The Falcon Wing Press; Indian Hills, Colorado, 1956

Breasted, James Henry. *A History of Egypt*, Charles Scribner's Sons; New York, 1912

Possehl, Gregory L., Editor. *Harrappan Civilization, a Contemporary Perspective*, Aris & Phillips LTD; Warminster, England, 1982

The Cambridge Ancient History, Vol. I, Part II. "The Early History of the Middle East", edited by I.E.S. Edwards, C.J. Gad, N.G.L. Hammond, E. Sollberger, Cambridge at the University Press; London, England, 1973

The Cambridge Ancient History, Vol. VII. "The Hellenistic Monarchies and The rise of Rome", edited by S.A. Cook, E.E. Adcock, M.D. Charlesworth Cambridge at the University Press, London, England, 1964

Durant, Will. *The Story of Civilization, Vol. 1, Our Oriental Heritage*, Simon and Schuster, New York, 1963

Durant, Will. *The Story of Civilization, Vol 2, The life of Greece*, Simon and Schuster, New York, 1966

Bury, J.B. "*A History of Greece*, The Modern Library, Published by Random House, Inc.; New York

Modern Religion In The Near East And Rome

Durant, Will. *The Story of Civilization*, Vol. 3, "Caesar and Christ", Simon and Schuster; New York, 1972

Gibbon, Edward. *The History of the Decline and Fall of the Roman Empire*, Volumes I thru V, Potter & Coates; Philadelphia

Rogers, Robert William. *A History of Ancient Persia*, Charles Scribner's Sons; New York, London, 1929

Olmstead, A.T. *History of Assyria*, The University of Chicago Press; Chicago 1951

The Cambridge Ancient History, Vol. IV, "The Persian Empire and the West." Edited by J.B. Bury, S.A. Cook, F.E. Adcock; Cambridge at the University Press, London 1964

The Cambridge Ancient History, Vol. III, "The Assyrian Empire", edited by J.B. Bury, S.A. Cook, F.E. Adcock; Cambridge at the University Press London, 1965

The Cambridge Ancient History, Vol. VIII, "Rome and the Mediterranean 218-133 B.C.", edited by S.A. Cook, F.E. Adcock, M.P. Charlesworth, Cambridge at the University Press; London 1965

The Cambridge Ancient History, Vol. IX, "The Roman Republic 133-44 B.C. Edited by S.A. Cook, F.E. Adcock, M. P. Charlesworth, Cambridge at the University Press, London, 1932

Great Religions of Modern Man, "Judaism", edited by Arthur Hertzberg, George Braziller; New York, 1962

The New English Bible with the Apocrypha, Oxford University Press; Cambridge University Press, 1970

Russell, Bertrand, *A History of Western Philosophy*, Simon and Schuster; New York, 1972

Christianity, Persia And Islam

Great Religions of Modern Man: "Islam", edited by John Alden Williams, George Braziller; New York, 1962

Great Religions of Modern Man: "Catholicism", edited by George Branntl, George Braziller; New York, 1962

The Cambridge History of Islam, Vol. I, edited by P.M. Holt, Ann K.S. Lambton Bernard Lewis, Cambridge at the University Press; London, 1970

Durant, Will, *The Story of Civilization*, Vol. 4, "The Age of Faith", Simon and Schuster; New York, 1950

The Cambridge Medieval History, Vol. I, "The Christian Roman Empire and the Foundations of the Teutonic Kingdoms", planned by J.B. Bury, edited by H.M. Gwatkin, J.P. Whitney, The Macmillan Co.; New York, 1911

The Cambridge Medieval History, Vol. II, "The Rise of the Saracens and the Foundation of the Eastern Empire", planned by J.B. Bury, edited by H.M. Gwatkin, J.P. Whitney, The Macmillan Co.; New York, 1913

Great Books of the Western World, Vol. 18, "The Confessions", "The City Of God", "On Christian Doctrine", by Saint Augustine, William Benton Publisher, Enclyclopaedia Britannica, Inc.; Chicago, 1952

Modern Religious Thought And The Birth Of Atheism

The Cambridge Modern History, Vol. I, "The Renaissance", edited by A.W. Ward, Sir G.W. Prothero, Sir Stanley Leathes, The Macmillan Co.; New York, 1934

The Cambridge Modern History, Vol. II, "The Reformation", ibid. The Macmillan Co.; New York, 1934

The Cambridge Modern History, Vol. VI, "The Eighteenth Century", ibid., The Macmillan Co.; New York, 1934

The Cambridge Modern History, Vol. XI, "The growth of Nationalities", Ibid, The Macmillan Co.; New York, 1934

Durant, Will, *The Story of Civilization*, Vol. 5, "The Renaissance", Simon and Schuster; New York, 1953

Durant, Will and Ariel, *The Story of Civilization*, Vol. 6, "The Reformation", Simon and Schuster; New York, 1957

Great Religions of Modern Man, "Protestantism", edited by J. Leslie Dunstan, George Braziller; New York, 1962

Atheism As A Positive Social Force

The New English Bible with the Apocrypha, Oxford University Press, Cambridge University Press, 1970

Struve, Otto, *The Universe*, The M.I.T. Press; Cambridge, MA, 1962

Orgel, L.E., *The Origins of Life: Molecules and Natural Selection*, John Wiley & Sons; New York, 1973

Popper, Karl R., *The Logic of Scientific Discovery*, Harper Torchbooks, The Science Library, Harper & Row, Publishers; New York, 1965

Tindall, George Brown, Shi, David E., *America, A Narrative History*, Fourth Edition, W.W. Norton &Company; New York, London, 1984

Atheism In The U.S.

Tindall, George Brown, Shi, David E., *America, A Narrative History*, Fourth Edition, W.W. Norton & Company; New York, London, 1984

The History of the United States, Vol. I, and II. "1600-1876 Source Readings", and "1850 to the Present", edited by Neil Harris, David J. Rothman, Stephan Thernstrom, Holt, Rinehart, Winston, Inc.; New York, 1960

Hume's Moral and Political Philosophy, edited by Henry D. Aiken, Hafner Publishing Co.; New York, 1966

Atheism As The Arbiter Of Social Self-Interest

Popper, Karl R., *The Logic of Scientific Discovery*, Harper Torchbooks, The Science Library, Harper & Row Publishers; New York, 1965

Popper, Karl R., *The Open Society and its Enemies*, Vol. I & II, Harper Torchbooks, The Academy Library, Harper & Row Publishers; New York, 1966

The Task Of Atheism

Great Books of the Western World, Vol. 54, "Freud, Civilization and its Discontents", PG 767, translated by Joan Reviere, Robert Maynard Hutchins, editor in chief, William Benton. Enclyclopaedia Britannica, Inc.; Chicago 1952

Tindall, George Brown, Shi, David E., *America, A Narrative History*", Fourth Edition, W.W. Norton & Company; New York, London, 1984

Moore, G.E., *Principia Ethica*, Cambridge University Press; Cambridge, 1991

Printed in the United States
23113LVS00001B/191

9 780875 862118